Relational Theology

RELATIONAL THEOLOGY
A Contemporary Introduction

Co-Editors:
Brint Montgomery
Thomas J. Oord
Karen Strand Winslow

WIPF & STOCK · Eugene, Oregon

RELATIONAL THEOLOGY
A Contemporary Introduction

Point Loma Press Series

Point Loma Press
3900 Lomaland Dr.
San Diego, CA 92106

Wipf and Stock Publishers
199 W. 8th Ave., Suite 3
Eugene, OR 97401
www.wipfandstock.com

ISBN 13: 978-1-62032-744-9

Contents

II. Biblical Witness in Relational Perspective

III. The Christian Life in Relational Perspective

IV. Ethics and Justice in Relational Perspective

Foreword for Point Loma Press Series

Point Loma Press was founded in 1992 to provide a publishing outlet for faculty and to serve the distinct theological mission of Point Loma Nazarene University (San Diego, CA). Over time the press has grown to publish authors from a wider range of institutional backgrounds, but its core mission remains the same: to encourage and extend a distinctly Wesleyan theological perspective on various topics and issues for the church today. Most Point Loma Press books are theological in scope, though many are quite practical in their focus, and some address non-theological topics but from a Wesleyan theological perspective. All Point Loma Press books are written with a broad audience in mind, intended to contribute effectively to contemporary scholarship while also being accessible to pastors, laypersons, and students alike. Our hope is that our new collaboration with Wipf & Stock Publishers will continue to allow us to expand our audience for the important topics and perspective of our work.

Point Loma Press welcomes any submissions that meet these criteria. Inquiries should be directed to PointLomaPress@pointloma.edu or 619-849-2359. When submitting, please provide rationale for how your work supports the mission of the Point Loma Nazarene University Wesleyan Center to articulate distinctly Wesleyan themes and trajectories.

For Emily, Cheryl, and Dale

Acknowledgments

The editors would like to thank the many authors who graciously agreed to be a part of this project. Often they were called upon to make additional revisions, and all did so quickly and efficiently.

We must mention Mark Mann for his coordination and support of this project. It takes a person with both intellect and vision to shepherd such a venture, and he has shown courage in advocating for relational theology. We would also be remiss if we didn't thank the Point Loma Press staff for preparing the work for publication. Finally, we would like to thank our spouses to whom this book is dedicated.

Contributors

Dean Blevins is Professor of Practical Theology and Christian Discipleship and Director of Master of Arts program in Christian Formation and Discipleship at Nazarene Theological Seminary, Kansas City, Missouri.

Dennis Bratcher is Executive Director of CRI/Voice, Institute http://www.crivoice.org

Barry L. Callen is Dean and Professor Emeritus at Anderson University, Anderson, Indiana, and Editor of the Wesleyan Theological Journal.

Charles J. Conniry, Jr., is Vice President and Dean at George Fox Evangelical Seminary, a graduate school of George Fox University, Portland, Oregon.

Timothy J. Crutcher is Professor of Church History and Theology at Southern Nazarene University, Bethany, Oklahoma.

T. Scott Daniels is Dean of Azusa Pacific School of Theology and Pastor of Pasadena First Church of the Nazarene, Pasadena, California.

Derek Flood, M.A., is a writer, artist and theologian. Flood is a featured blogger for the religious section of the Huffington Post.

Philip R. Hamner is Senior Pastor of the Overland Park Church of the Nazarene, Overland Park, Kansas.

Douglas S. Hardy is Professor of Spiritual Formation at Nazarene Theological Seminary, Kansas City, Missouri.

Sharon R. Harvey is Faculty Lecturer and General Studies Program Director at Arizona State University, Lake Havasu City, Arizona, and teaches for the Environmental Science Program at University of Idaho, Moscow, Idaho.

Wm. Curtis Holtzen is Associate Professor of Philosophy and Theology at Hope International University, Fullerton, California.

Diane Leclerc is Professor of Historical Theology at Northwest Nazarene University, Nampa, Idaho.

Michael Lodahl is Professor of Theology and World Religions at Point Loma Nazarene University, San Diego, California.

Kevin Twain Lowery is Professor of Theology and Philosophy at Olivet Nazarene University, Bourbonnais, Illinois.

Mark H. Mann is Director of the Wesleyan Center and Point Loma Press at Point Loma Nazarene University and Associate Pastor of Peace River Christian Fellowship, San Diego, California.

K. Steve McCormick, is Professor of Historical Theology and William M. Greathouse Chair for Wesleyan-Holiness Theology at Nazarene Theological Seminary, Kansas City, Missouri.

Marty Alan Michelson is a Peacemaker, Pastor, and Professor at Southern Nazarene University, Bethany, Oklahoma.

Brint Montgomery is Professor of Philosophy at Southern Nazarene University, Bethany, Oklahoma.

Thomas Jay Oord is Professor of Theology and Philosophy at Northwest Nazarene University, Nampa, Idaho and blogs frequently at http://thomasjayoord.com.

Brent D. Peterson is Associate Professor of Theology at Northwest Nazarene University, Nampa, Idaho.

Brian Postlewait is CEO of Mission Possible, a Nazarene Compassionate Ministry Center in Vancouver BC.

Samuel M. Powell is Professor of Philosophy and Religion at Point Loma Nazarene University, San Diego, California.

Jeren Rowell is pastor to the pastors—District Superintendant—of the Kansas City District Church of the Nazarene, Kansas City, Missouri.

Gabriel Salguero is the President of the National Latino Evangelical Coalition, Lead Pastor of The Lamb's Church, New York.

R. Larry Shelton is Professor of Theology at George Fox Evangelical Seminary, Portland, Oregon.

Dwight D. Swanson is Senior Research Fellow in Biblical Studies at Nazarene Theological College, Manchester, England.

Libby P. Tedder is a minister in Casper, Wyoming.

Richard P. Thompson is Professor of New Testament at Northwest Nazarene University, Nampa, Idaho.

Karen Strand Winslow is Professor of Biblical Studies/Free Methodist Center Director at Azusa Pacific Graduate School of Theology, Azusa, California.

Amos Yong is J. Rodman Williams Professor of Theology at Regent University in Virginia Beach, Virginia.

Introduction

What is Relational Theology?

Thomas Jay Oord

In recent days, many Christians are finding the ideas and language of relational theology helpful. As they read the Bible, Christians frequently encounter relational theology's ideas and language. Unfortunately, however, conventional Christian theologies have sometimes ignored relational ideas and language. The theology that results is sometimes impractical and nonsensical.

The Bible describes the activities and nature of a relational God. This relational God created "in the beginning" and invited creatures to "bring forth" others in creative activity. God's interactions with Adam and Eve portray God as relational. From the beginning, God instructs, expects, and responds to creatures—all of which are relational activities.

The Bible says God makes covenants with Israel and all creation. God's covenant making demonstrates God's relationality. Because God is relational, sinful behavior makes God angry. But positive responses and ongoing relationship deepens the relational friendship God shares with creatures. God is pleased. Biblical authors repeatedly proclaim that a God of steadfast love never gives up on the relationship that God initiates and seeks to develop.

In Jesus Christ, the relational God is specially incarnated. In him, we have the fullest revelation of God as relational. Jesus teaches that God is our Abba (Father), an intimately relational description. God calls us to enter into a mutually loving relationship—what Jesus announces as the greatest commandment. Jesus reinforces Old Testament themes about the importance of love relations. Christians are commanded to love believers and unbelievers, friends and enemies, the near and dear as well as the stranger.

The Christian community emerging soon after God raised Jesus from the dead was Holy Spirit empowered. This budding community emphasized from its inception the importance of interrelatedness. As the Church, they ate together and shared things in common. They worshipped and prayed together. They shared the Lord's Supper as a community. Christians embarked as the Church on a give-and-receive mission of relational love.

If God created a relational universe and relational people, it should come as little surprise that recent developments in science, philosophy, and culture reveal the interrelatedness of all existence. Relationality profoundly shapes personal and social levels of existence. And relational perspectives influence scientific research of the distant edges of our cosmos.

What makes relational theology distinct is its general approach to thinking about God's interaction with creation. At its core, relational theology affirms two key ideas:

1. God affects creatures in various ways. Instead of being aloof and detached, God is active and involved in relationship with others. God relates to us, and that makes an essential difference.

2. Creatures affect God in various ways. While God's nature is unchanging, creatures influence the loving and living Creator of the universe. We relate to God, and creation makes a difference to God.

Of course, those who embrace relational theology typically embrace other theological ideas too. For instance, many think God's primary attribute is love, and many believe God's chief desire is that people love others as themselves. Most think God relates within Trinity, and Jesus Christ best reveals God's relational love. Most think God and creatures are genuinely free, at least to some degree. Most emphasize the importance of relationships in the Church, outside the Church, and relationships with all creation. Most think relational categories are central to Christian ethics and should be guides to get along with others—both human and nonhuman—on our planet. The list of other theologically important ideas continues.

People interpret variously what the two main ideas of relational theology entail. Because of these diverse interpretations, relational theology is like a big umbrella idea under which various theological alternatives reside. We might illustrate the umbrella like this:

RELATIONAL THEOLOGY

Various Theologies

Missional	Arminian & Holiness	Feminist/ Womanist	Open	Trinitar- ian	Process	Wesleyan	Liberation/ Postcolonial	Other

(This chart applies to most, or many, but not all variations of these theological alternatives.) Some people adopt one theological alternative but reject another under the relational umbrella. For instance, some people adopt Trinitarian theology as the primary way they think about Christian theology but reject Process theology. Others embrace both Trinitarian and Process theologies. Or some feminist theologians do not identify as Arminian, but others do. A person need not embrace all theologies under the umbrella. But these theologies share the ideas about God and creatures being relational.

It is also important to note that some theologians embrace a number of theological traditions simultaneously. For instance, a person might say she is Wesleyan, liberation, process, and Trinitarian. Another person might say he is Arminian, missional, and open. Still others might embrace one theology and not another listed above. And further, even others might be Process, Emergent, and Pentecostal. Many other combinations exist.

Confusion sometimes emerges when people identify relational theology with personalities or character traits we might consider "relational." People who are friendly, sociable, or highly empathetic do not necessarily embrace the ideas of relational theology. Of course, we usually hope people develop adequate social sensibilities. But a relational theologian is not automatically an expert at relating to other people!

To the extent that Christians seek to be Christ-like, however, relational theology can encourage loving interactions and character traits that promote positive relationships. We best understand the Apostle Paul's command to "imitate God, as dearly loved children, and live a life of love as Christ loved us..." (Eph 5:1, 2), for instance, in relational terms. Those who consistently heed Paul's counsel develop into the kind of people we call "virtuous" or "saints."

We could say much more about the implications of relational theology. In fact, that's exactly what this book is about: exploring the implications of relational theology.

Our book doesn't cover every conceivable topic, of course. And people who adopt relational theology may come to differing conclusions about how an issue might best be understood. Despite these limitations, this book should help us explore how we might think, live, and minister well from a relational theology framework.

The book's contributors come from a variety of ministerial and educational backgrounds. They represent a small portion of those who embrace relational theology. We hope you find their contributions helpful in your own thinking and living in relation with a loving God and others. We want this book to be pondered, discussed, and evaluated. Toward that end, we've asked some contributors to write short pieces to encourage this kind of reflection. We hope this material proves helpful for various kinds of groups, interactions, and community gatherings.

I.
Doctrines of Theology in Relational Perspective

John Wesley and Relational Theology
Barry L. Callen

Relational theology is a contemporary movement in the broader Evangelical Christian world. It seeks to react biblically to perceived weaknesses in much current theology. The task here is to place relational theology alongside the Wesleyan revival of eighteenth-century England, particularly the theology of John Wesley. We are looking for natural connections and obvious similarities.

A caution and affirmation are in order. Linking a current movement with an older one is risky business. It is easy to equate things from different settings and times when they were not as similar as may appear on the surface. Even so, there is a legitimate affirmation. The characteristic stances of the Wesleyan revival do bear considerable similarity to the current relational theology movement.

Identifying these stances has two values. First, it helps Christians in the Wesleyan tradition to reconsider their theology in the context of today's thinking. Second, it reassures those doing relational theology today that their concerns and insights are not novel. Relational theology has deep and honorable roots in the Bible and church history.

Relational theology has roots in the Pietist, Arminian, Wesleyan, Holiness, and Pentecostal traditions of Christianity. The focus of these roots lies in the interactivity or mutuality of the God-human relationship. God is understood to be truly personal, loving, and not manipulative. The interaction of the wills of Creator and creature is real. In contrast to the Reformed or Calvinistic tradition that features a more static and predetermined God-creature relationship, the relational tradition emphasizes the responsive compassion of the sovereign God.

7

John Wesley viewed God as having a dynamic constancy of character. It is neither a divine immutability nor raw omnipotence, but a living sovereignty of love. It is like that vital question posed by Scrooge, the character in "A Christmas Carol" by Charles Dickens. In reference to an ugly tombstone, Scrooge asks, "Are these the shadows of things that *will be* or are they the shadows of things that *may be only*?" He wanted to know if the future is still in the making and whether a change of life on his part could still make a difference. He hoped for a future of fresh possibilities, for an "open" view of God—and he found it!

Such a relational view affirms that divine sovereignty—rather than separating and suffocating—embraces the possibility of the creature actively cooperating in God's governance of this creation. God loves, reaches, relates, and responds to repentant and prayerful believers. A relational God has created relational people in a relational world.

John Wesley began by following a personalistic (biblical) rather than an absolutistic (philosophical) conception of God. For Wesley, reports Clark Pinnock, "it was not so much God as creator, judge, and king, with the emphasis on divine control and unchangeability, as it was on God as saviour, lover, and friend, with the emphasis on relationality and [human] response-ability. Wesley viewed God not as a unilateral power that takes no risks, but as a bilateral power which gives creatures room."[1] God's grace works powerfully, but not irresistibly, in matters of human life and salvation. God empowers our "response-ability" without overriding our genuine responsibility. Human beings must be co-laborers with God in the great work of redemption.

Wesley did not participate in the theological debate as currently framed. However, the heart of his reform involved a vision of God similar to one of the relational theologians today. The eighteenth-century debate Wesley participated in involved a key question: Does God respond to us humans by doing things *because of us* and not merely *through us*? For instance, can prayer really make a difference in God's actions? Wesley insisted on a "yes" answer. He focused on divine love, the plan of salvation, and the transforming work of the Spirit of God. While there are no limits to God's power, we should not define divine power in any way that undercuts human responsibility in the salvation process. According to

---

1   Clark Pinnock, "The Beauty of God: John Wesley's Reform and Its Aftermath," *Wesleyan Theological Journal* (Fall 2003): 58.

Wesley, God's justifying and regenerating graces are neither irresistible nor coercive.

The orienting concern of Wesley appears highly compatible with a relational theology. The challenge is to preserve the vital tension between two truths that Wesley viewed as co-definitive of Christianity. They are (1) without God's grace, we *cannot* be saved, and (2) without our grace-empowered but uncoerced participation, God's grace *will not* save. The first of these truths is Wesley's Protestant emphasis (it is God *alone*) and the second might be called his Catholic emphasis (it is also *human cooperation* with divine activity).

Only God's grace can forgive sinners and make them holy. However, adding the relational element, sinners must actively receive such grace in an uncoerced, responsible, and accountable way. The fullness of this dual perspective is this. Salvation is by grace only, but also with responsible reception of that grace. This fullness of perspective for Wesley came through his commitment to the heritage of the Church of England, with its rich Reformation tradition and its strong sense of catholicity. The resulting Wesleyan heritage assumes that God expects cooperation by believers. We have been granted the freedom of choice necessary to cooperate with divine grace or to resist it. Divine coercion (predestination) is not God's way.

Wesley understood that proper relationships are central to true salvation and intended human existence. He understood that, by sheer grace, God has given us the capacity for right relationships. "Prevenient" grace comes before and enables our faith response. It is God's initial move toward the potential righting of relationships with a fallen humanity. This enabling grace allows a real role for humans in the salvation process, although a role that is always grounded in God's gracious empowering, not in any inherent human ability or merit-earning "works."

The stress on sanctification makes clear that Wesley centered much of his thought on the *present reality* of our life in God. It shows his openness to the enabling gifts of the Spirit for maturing our faith and inspiring effective ministry. This strong belief in relationality, however, does not allow openness to go to seed in individualism. For Wesley, the fellowship of the church is essential, both in its historic tradition and through "class meetings" with their intimacy, discipline, and mutual care, support, and accountability. He fought barriers to Christian unity by insisting that joining the early Methodist fellowships did not require agreement on all doctrinal matters or modes of worship. It required only reverence for God and willingness to work with God and fellow believers to further righteousness.

For John Wesley and current relational theologians, there appears to be a common bottom line. Christian spirituality is a cooperative enterprise. All praise to God who *reigns above* and *responds below*!

The "Way" of Triune Love

K. Steve McCormick

The focus of this essay is to pinpoint in the biblical narrative the "way" God speaks and dwells in creation. The "way" God is "in all" and "for all" creation is the patterned, ordered, and structured "way" for all creation to dwell in God, as God dwells in all creation. God has made this "way" to be "all in all" so that in the end, all that God has created will be in all of God. God will be "all in all" (1 Cor 15:28). This is the beginning of God's promise of new creation, which is the deification (Greek, *theosis*) of all creation.

Inspired from the biblical story, Charles Wesley declared in poetry that God's "name and nature is love." According to the biblical witness, God has spoken most definitively through the Son who is the radiance of God's glory and the exact imprint of God's very being (Heb 1:1). It was God's Son who taught us to call his God, "Abba Father." It was God's Spirit who poured the energy of God's love into our hearts (Rom 5:5) enabling us to cry, in the Spirit of our Lord, "Abba Father" (Rom 8:15).

In the fullness of time, God named Godself through the Son and the Spirit. The name of God's self-giving is Father, Son, and Holy Spirit. God comes to dwell in us in the self-naming, humbling love of God, so that we may dwell in God. In the self-giving, self-emptying "way" that God comes to dwell in all creation by making room (Hebrew, *makom*) in all of God, all of creation may dwell in all of God.

This "way" of God's indwelling and outflowing love is depicted in John Wesley's vision of the *Scripture Way of Salvation* that is our "hope of glory." For Wesley, God's abundant, endless, overflowing and indwelling love, is the "way" that we are made "capable of God." In this patterned way of salvation, we may become partakers of God. We become by God's gracious indwelling what God is in name and nature (2 Pet 1:4). In other words, the "way" God is "for us and our salvation" is the very "way" in which we partake of God's nature and become a reflection of Triune love by God's constant giving and receiving love.

This "way" of God's constant giving and receiving opens a window into the very heart of God. It reveals to all creation that the name and nature of God is love. The heart of God is not unlike the human heart that continuously contracts and expands. As our hearts beat, they contract to pump in (*diastole*) life-giving blood and oxygen. And they expand to pump out (*systole*) the same life-giving blood and oxygen. Similarly, with every heartbeat of God, God is constantly contracting and expanding, emptying and filling, indwelling and overflowing, giving and receiving.

This metaphor of the heart illumines the "way" of Triune Love. As God comes to dwell with us and in us, God makes space and room for us to dwell in the heart of God. This profound "way" of God's space making is the "way" of God's nature, God's love. God's overflowing and indwelling love has made space and room for us to dwell in God, in the very "way" that God the Father, Son, and Holy Spirit make room and space for one another.

The biblical story is replete with the concrete and embodied ways of illustrating God's "way" of making space. By the constant reciprocal indwelling of God the Father, Son, and Holy Spirit contracting and expanding to make room and dwell totally in each other, we see that the "way" of God's indwelling unity is the space-making *way* of Triune Love.

The story of God's love is told in the concrete and unfolding scenes of the Gospels. The thread weaving those scenes into the full tapestry of Triune Love is like a riddle woven into the very fabric of the gospel. The tale of this riddle could be: *wherever the Son is, there is the Spirit, and wherever the Spirit is, there is the Son.* Whatever the Son can do, he can do only by the power of the Spirit. Whatever the Spirit can do, can only be done through the life, death, and resurrection of the Son. Whatever the Son and the Spirit do, they always do according to the character and mission of God. This is the space-making "way" of Triune Love.

The space-making "way" of God in Christ and the Spirit comes to us wrapped in the enigma of love that "is" God. That is to say, God is abundant outpouring love, and the will of God in the mission of the

Spirit is always to "pour out . . . on all flesh" (Joel 2:28; Acts 2:17), all living creation, the abundant energy of love that is God. For in the *fullness* of God's mission, Christ and the Spirit revealed that God *is* love. The mission of the gospel is born out of the very heart of God. Throughout the grand narrative of God's mission is this enduring riddle of self-giving love: *wherever the Spirit is, there is the Son, and wherever the Son is, there is the Spirit.* The Spirit's mission is to breathe the life, energy and love of God on all flesh, all living creation until God is "all in all."

The mission of Christ and the Spirit is the way of God making space in all creation in the "way" of Triune Love. *God's name and nature is Love.* As we wait for the promise of new creation when God is "all in all," let us live in the hope of glory with the poetry of Charles Wesley in our hearts: "And when we rise in love renewed, Our souls resemble Thee, and image of the Triune God to all eternity."[1]

---

1   Charles Wesley, "For Believers Rejoicing," §248:6, *The Bicentennial Edition of The Works of John Wesley* (Nashville: Abingdon, 1984–) 7:390.

The Person and Work of Christ
R. Larry Shelton

S ome time ago, a friend of mine who is a rescue diver with the Fire
Department Search and Rescue team geared up for an evidence
dive in an investigation. As he explored the bottom of a frigid river,
his dive gear failed, drastically reducing his air supply. Later, after he was
rescued, his friends asked him, "What were you thinking in this terrifying
experience?" He said, "Air. I was thinking only about finding air."

This was the crisis of humanity when Jesus arrived on earth. It was
with a breath of air God first breathed life into humanity and began
humanity's relationship with God and the rest of Creation. And it
was with the arrogance of belief in its own independence from God
that humanity found itself alienated from its Creator. Humans were
desperately in need of the life-giving air of the Spirit of God, the Giver
of Life.

The Person of Christ

With the birth of Jesus of Nazareth, God's mystery of salvation began
to take shape. In the story of the Holy Spirit creating new life in Mary's
womb, the Spirit who first collaborated with Adam to create Eve now
collaborates with a teen-age woman, Mary, to re-conceive humanity
in the baby Jesus. The Life-Giver who inspired creation again breathes
life into humanity. This Life-Giver also becomes intimately linked with
humanity in the conception of Jesus. The Creator, who breathed life into
the archetypal first man with a kiss, now conceives life in an archetypal
first woman to create a new humanity. And, in the birth of Jesus, the
Word of Creation becomes in Christ the Word of Life. As Christ takes

on human life as a new Adam—obedience rather than disobedience leads to a restoration of intimacy with the source of life.

Jesus not only lived as a man. He also taught humans how to live. His model of wisdom, love, and obedience to God paints the picture of a new humanity who lives in covenant relationship and obedience to God in the way the Creator intended humans to live.

The Mission of Christ

Adam's story is one of choosing to withdraw from intimacy with the Creator, his very source of breath and life (Gen 3:1–24). As if this story needed further evidence of bad judgment, Adam blames his wife—his first anti-relational act! As the deprivation of breath results in deterioration of the life cells, so the decay of the covenant relationship for which humanity was created began its downward moral spiral of self-destruction.

Humanity's sin is represented in the story of Adam and Eve's transgression of God's command, "Do not eat the fruit of this tree of the Knowledge of Good and Evil" (Gen 2:17). God created humanity to be in responsible relationship with him, and to find its identity—the "image of God"—in relationship. Yet humanity sought to become independent of its Creator and claim self-sufficiency.

This was a denial of community and covenant relationship as the foundation of life. Humanity's separation, or deprivation, from the source of life resulted in a downward spiral that led not only to the destruction, or depravation, of the covenant community with God. It also led to the destruction of the natural ecosystem and humanity's relationship with nature.

Christ's mission, then, was to become the New Adam (Rom 4 and 5). Christ acts to restore humanity's divine image and covenant relationship with its Creator. In Christ, we find that salvation is restored friendship with God.

The Work of Christ

Christ's work was to identify with and participate in humanity through his incarnation ("in the flesh"). Christ acts to re-breathe the breath of life into humanity as a restoration of humanity's creation.

Christ took into his own soul and body the suffering, brokenness, and alienation of humanity. He fully participated in it to the point of taking its own death upon himself on the cross. Crucifixion is about asphyxiation—the body's ability to breathe is disabled. Christ shared in this existential dying and alienation of all humanity.

The asphyxiation of the cross-death became a parable of the life of humanity that began with the Spirit's kiss and the light of Creation. The parable ended with a Roman cross and the fury of nature's darkness (Lk 23:44). Christ took on the consequences of humanity's choice to depend on itself rather than on its divine source of breath. God's Spirit restores life to the humanity that was doomed by its own moral asphyxiation.

If we simply look at Christ's atonement as a legal transaction that satisfies humanity's penalty for sin, we miss much of what Christ has accomplished for us. What Christ did was highly personal. Above all, it restored our personal relationship and union with our creator God.

Our belief isn't merely that we are now free to live our lives because the deal has been done for us. Our belief is that God has called us to enter into a covenant relationship with him and, furthermore, to enter into his mission (Jn 4:13–16). This offers insights into the pastoral applications of Christ's work as the re-establishment of our covenant relationship with God.

The Resurrection of Christ

Christ's death was not the last word. That last word was spoken on Easter morning when Christ's tomb was found empty. "Death starts working backwards," as C.S. Lewis describes Aslan's awakening, and the testimony, "He is risen," echoes through the Jerusalem dawn.

As the God-Man, Christ fully takes on human life as the new Adam. His obedience rather than humanity's disobedience leads to a restoration of its intimacy with the source of life (Rom 8:11).

The resurrection is the Holy Spirit giving life to our as-good-as-dead bodies by her new life-breath. Our newly restored relationship with the life in the Spirit replaces our former alienation from the Creator (Rom 8). Jesus came to correct Adam's mistake and show us how to live in a true relationship of union with God. God is love, and if we truly live in relationship with God, we will live in love with others and all creation.

Conclusion

Relational theology emphasizes the centrality of love for effective pastoral application of one's relationship with God. The effective use of the relational biblical covenant concept thus results in a radically relational understanding of the Christian life. This is based solidly in the relational-covenantal concepts of the Trinity, creation community, and Israel's covenant history.

The restoration of nature cannot be separated from our own human restoration, because humanity's job was originally to take care of creation (Gen 1:28–30). Christ's resurrection provides the beginnings of a new creation. And as the relational community of faith, the Church as Christ's body seeks and expresses the restoration of humanity's harmony with all Creation (Rom 8:18–25).

Relational Theology and the Holy Spirit
Amos Yong

The doctrine of the Holy Spirit lies at the very heart of relational theology. In this chapter, we will note the relational aspects of the Holy Spirit in multiple dimensions: in the very life of the loving, Trinitarian God; in God's relationship with the world; in the very fabric of the world itself; and in the world's ultimate reconciliation with God.

We begin with the Trinitarian mystery of God as Father, Son, and Holy Spirit. This aspect of the Spirit's relationality is most obscure and speculative. But major theologians of the church, such as St. Augustine and Richard of St. Victor, have argued that the Spirit is the bond of love between the Father and the Son. In that sense, I invite us to think about the Spirit as the relational connection in the very depths of the Trinitarian life. In the Gospel accounts, a hint of this relationality is glimpsed in the baptism of Jesus, where the Spirit is manifest in the form of a dove alighting on Jesus even as the Father's voice came from heaven saying, "This is my beloved Son, in whom I am well pleased."

If the Spirit is at the center of the relational life of God, the Spirit is also central to God's relationship with the world. Early church theologians like Irenaeus held that the Father created the world with his "two hands"—the Word and the Spirit. If the Word of God structures the world and its creatures, the Spirit of God is the dynamic life force that infuses creativity and novelty into the rhythms of creation. The Spirit, or breath of God, brooded and hovered over the primordial waters, and

18

then instilled the creatures of the world, including humanity, with the breath of life. Thus, the life breath of the Spirit sustains living creatures and empowers the cosmic arrow of time.

But the Spirit is not only the relational bond in the natural and biological worlds. The Spirit is also the relationality that enables human communion. There are spiritual and social aspects to the human experience that cannot be reduced to the biological domain. These reflect the relational sociality that sets humanity off from other forms of life. No person is an island off to his or herself. Human beings find meaning, fulfillment, and significance precisely in relationship to one another, bonded together by the common creator Spirit.

The Spirit of creation and of our common life together is also the Spirit of redemption and of our fellowship in Christ. Those who have come to recognize Jesus as the anointed Messiah—anointed by the Spirit to inaugurate the redemptive work of God in the world—are also given of the Spirit in the same way that he was. In a fallen world, the bonds of human communion have been broken and people are alienated from themselves, others, and their natural environments. But God's redeeming work consists of healing the estrangement of our hearts, reconciling human beings with one another, and restoring harmony between humanity and the cosmos.

How does the Spirit do this? First, by empowering Jesus of Nazareth to inaugurate the kingdom of God. Then by being poured out upon and made available to all flesh and filling human hearts so that the Spirit might work from within human lives, touching our inmost beings with the love of God. All of this is done so that we can now love others in turn. Ultimately, the same Spirit of Christ who transforms our hate into love is the Spirit sent on the Day of Pentecost who empowers us to take this message of love to others. This Spirit enables us to bear witness to the healing power of love, even to the ends of the earth.

The redemptive work of the Spirit begun in Christ and poured out on the world at Pentecost is what the apostolic followers of Jesus called the Spirit of the last days (Acts 2:17). The Spirit of creation is now the Spirit of the kingdom that has already dawned in Christ but yet to be fully unveiled only in the end.

The Spirit is the bridge between our present life in Christ and the future fullness of the kingdom of Christ. In the Spirit, we live both now and in the future, both in the presence of the kingdom in some way and yet in hopes for the kingdom in other ways. The Spirit enables us to do the works of the kingdom now. But the Spirit also enables us to pray for the coming kingdom. In other words, the Spirit relates our present time, the time of the process of redemption, with the future time of God when all of creation will be renewed.

All of the preceding provide windows into the centrality of the Holy Spirit in relational theology. Relationality is what reality is all about, because it characterizes the very life of the Triune God who is spirit and whose Holy Spirit is the bond of love between the Father and the Son. God is also related to the world through the Word and the Spirit. The world is interrelated creationally through the Spirit, even as life itself is a relational dynamic of the Spirit.

There is more good news: the relational Spirit has come to restore creaturely relations—with one another, with the world, and with God. Hence, the world, and human beings within it, now have a glimpse of the relational kingdom of God through the Spirit who has been shed abroad in human hearts. We can anticipate, even now, the day when Creation itself will become the all-encompassing dwelling place of God in the Spirit of divine love.

Participation in God
Charles J. Conniry, Jr.

A book on relational theology requires at least a brief reflection on the concept of "participation in God." Relationality begins and ends with God. God exists in relationship—the Trinity. Through the act of creation, God extended relationality to all God made. And in the coming age, redeemed humanity will share in Christ's glory—a glory that includes the creation "liberated from its bondage to decay and brought into the glorious freedom of the children of God" (see Rom 8:17–21).

There are at least two ways to conceive of relational participation in God. Stated in theological shorthand, they are (1) panentheism and (2) theosis.

Panentheism

The term panentheism simply means "everything" (*pan*) "in" (*en*) "God" (*theos*). It is based on the doctrine of God's "omnipresence" (God is everywhere). When the psalmist exclaims, "Where can I go from your Spirit? Where can I flee from your presence? If I go up to the heavens, you are there; if I make my bed in the depths, you are there" (Ps 139:7, 8), he is making a statement about God's *everywhereness*. The apostle Paul makes the same claim: "There is ... one God and Father of all, who is over all and through all and in all" (Eph 4:6).

This means relationally that God's embrace envelops us. In God "we live and move and have our being" (Acts 17:28). God is, in a word, near, because God *wants* to be in a relationship with us. Paul says in Acts 17 that God determined the boundaries and duration of nations in order for them "to seek after God and perhaps feel their way toward him and find him—*though he is not far from any one of us*" (v. 27, emphasis added).

The term panentheism makes some Christians nervous. Some confuse it with *pantheism*, which means, "God is all and all is God." That is not what panentheism means! Others struggle with the idea of God's relational proximity (God's immanence), because they think of *physical* and *spiritual* as two distinct spheres of existence that stay pretty much apart. This dualistic way of conceiving reality is due in part to the conditioning we've experienced as products of modern, Western culture.

What's fascinating, however, is that the Israelites viewed the physical and spiritual worlds as dynamically interconnected. They believed we perceive spiritual reality the same way we perceive physical reality: *through the five senses.* There are hundreds of passages in Hebrew Scripture that cite hearing, seeing, tasting, smelling, and touching as conduits through which we perceive the spiritual world.

The verb *to hear*, for example, occurs over a thousand times in the Bible and frequently describes discerning spiritual things. The same is true of the other verbs of perception. "*Taste* and *see* that the LORD is good," invites the psalmist (Ps 34:8).

This idea carried over into the New Testament. Jesus said to his disciples, "blessed are your eyes, because they see; and your ears, because they hear" (Mt 13:16). He was in this context describing the disciples' capacity to discern spiritual reality.

According to this Hebraic view of panentheism, we participate in relational union with God *by means of* our embodiedness, not in spite of it. God is all around us, in us, and through us—and yet God is not us and we are not God. We must tune in our various senses and participate with God.

Theosis

Theosis is the other word many use to talk about relational participation in God. Theosis comes from the Greek word that means, "becoming divine," and it refers to sharing in God's nature of love.

The idea of participating in God's divine nature took root early in Christian history. Irenaeus in the second century wrote that Jesus, the Son of God, became "human for this purpose, that humans also might become children of God." In almost identical fashion, Clement of

Alexandria said, "The Word of God became a man, that you may learn from a man how to become God." Similar statements are attributed to theologians throughout Christian history.

Theosis has implications for the way we live. It informs the way we behave and describes the nature of our existence. A key biblical passage is 2 Peter 1:3, 4, in which Peter announces that through God's great and precious promises, we have received all we need to live a godly life. These promises, says Peter, "enable you to share his divine nature and escape the world's corruption caused by human desires."

Another important theosis text is Genesis 1:26. It says humans were created in God's "image" and "likeness." Many early Christians said that despite sin, humans retain God's image but lost God's likeness. Through redemption in Christ and the sanctifying work of the Holy Spirit, human beings can share again in God's likeness.

There are both "now" and "then" aspects to theosis. In the present, we relate well with God when we behave in God-like ways. We are God's image bearers, and we reflect more and more of God's likeness in our day-to-day lives. In the life to come, we will realize the fullness of what it means to be co-heirs with Christ. As Jesus became like us in the incarnation, so in glory we will become like him (see Phil 3:20, 21).

Theosis doesn't mean we are like God in all ways. God is the uncreated Creator, for instance, but we are God's creation. In theosis, we do not become all knowing, omnipresent, or almighty. Only God has such attributes.

In sum, our participating with God is often thought of in at least two ways. Panentheism says God is with us all and we are enveloped in God's presence. And theosis calls us to imitate God now with the hope of sharing in God's glory in the future.

Relational Love
Thomas J. Oord

For some Christians, the issues of love are why they embrace relational theology. Love issues are central to the Bible and to who God is revealed to be. "God is love," says John (4:8, 16), and Old Testament authors repeatedly say God's love is everlastingly steadfast. Jesus says the first and second greatest commands are about love. Many find relational theology helpful for considering the love of Christ, love in the Church, love for enemies and outsiders, love of self, and God's love for all creation.

God Gives and Receives in Relationship

Love without relationship is impossible. This is especially clear in reciprocal relationships between friends, spouses, parents and children, and within communities. But it's also true of other relations. And this is one reason some Christians believe God is fundamentally relational.

Biblical authors often portray God as friend, husband, parent, judge, leader, lord, or king. These descriptions and others arise from God's relationality. God cannot be rightly called these names if not in relationship. In these descriptions and others, biblical writers explicitly or implicitly present God as in relationship with creation.

A relational God gives to but also receives from others. Creaturely love and obedience depends on God's initial loving activity. John put it this way, "We love, because he first loved us" (1 Jn 4:19). When creatures respond well to God's calls, God is pleased. When creatures fail to respond well, however, God is grieved, angry, and forgives. God's experience is affected by what creatures do. And God's decisions about how to act in one moment depend in part upon how creatures responded in previous moments.

24

God's relational love may seem eminently obvious. But not everyone has thought of God as relational. Aristotle famously rejected relational theology when he called God "the unmoved mover." By this phrase, he meant God "moves" others, but others do not "move" God. In other words, God is unaffected. According to Aristotle, God is invulnerable, impassible, and aloof. God does nothing but think about God's self.

The idea that God is unmoved by creatures influenced Christian theologians throughout the centuries. Because Augustine considered God not in reciprocal relationship with creatures, for instance, he could not imagine how God loves creatures. He believed God only loves himself. Thomas Aquinas called God "pure act" with no real give-and-receive relationship with creatures. Like a mighty fortress, God was considered impenetrable.

In the 20th century, theologians as liberal as Paul Tillich and as conservative as Carl Henry said divine perfection meant creatures could not influence God. God was considered in all ways unchanging and unaffected by others. Like an unresponsive monarch, God was considered uninfluenced by creatures.

Other Christians in the 20th and 21st centuries, however, believe God is better understood as relational. These believers agree with the contributors of this book that relational theology captures well the Bible's witness to a loving God in relationship with others.

Some Christians point to the Trinity as the best example of relational love. When Jesus says the Father is in him and he is in the Father (Jn 14:11) and that the Father loves the Son (Jn 5:20), Christians infer love relations exist within Trinity. This intra-Trinitarian love overflows to creation. Others point to God's love for creation as best describing the other-oriented nature of God's love.

What is Love?

When we say issues of love are central to relational theology, we should also describe as best we can what we mean by love. The word "love" has many meanings. It takes many forms, and we express love in a multitude of ways.

The confusion about love language is one reason some theologians do not take love as their central motif for understanding Christian faith. This is regrettable, because love is central to Christian understandings of

God, creation, salvation, ethics, ecclesiology, and a host of other issues. Relational theology better accounts for many facets of love in Christian theology.

Although no definition is likely to capture fully what we mean by love, I propose this one as better than others. I define love this way:

> *To love is to act intentionally, in response to God and others,*
> *to promote overall well-being.*

I have explained each phrase of this definition in other writings.[1] I focus here on the second phrase—"in response to God and others"— because it is especially important to relational theology.

We find in our own experience that knowing another person well is important for loving that person well. Well-informed relationships provide useful information when we consider how to be a blessing, be a source of comfort, or be helpful. Knowing another well is often crucial for loving that person well.

This principle applies to God's love, and this is one reason God loves perfectly. God knows everything about us and the whole universe. God's knowledge stems primarily from God's presence with us. As omnipresent, God directly knows all that occurs. As omniscient, God knows best what we need.

Unfortunately, some think of God as an all-seeing eye floating disconnected above creation. "God is watching us from a distance," to quote an old Bette Midler song. Rather than God being understood as relationally present to all creation, the "all seeing eye" view of God reinforces nonrelational views of deity. Instead of affirming it, we are better to agree with Apostle Paul that God's unsurpassing knowledge of us is possible, because "in him we live and move and have our being" (Acts 17:28).

Imitating God's Love

The role of love in relational theology is not limited to God's own love. Biblical passages say humans ought to love as God loves. The Apostle

---

1   I develop this definition in many books and articles, including *The Nature of Love: A Theology* (St. Louis, Mo.: Chalice, 2010), *Relational Holiness: Responding to the Call of Love*, with Michael Lodahl (Kansas City, Mo.: Beacon Hill, 2005), and *Defining Love: A Philosophical, Scientific, and Theological Engagement* (Grand Rapids, Mich.: Brazos, 2010).

Paul puts it like this: "Imitate God, as dearly loved children, and live a life of love as Christ loved you ..." (Eph 5:1). Many Christians argue that Christ-like love is at the heart of living the holy life.

Love takes diverse forms, and we express love in various ways. Christians sometimes use ancient Greek words—*agape, eros,* and *philia*—to talk about the forms of love God calls them to express. Other times, Christians point to particularly important expressions of love, such as forgiveness, friendship, self-sacrifice, compassion, self-control, acts of justice, affection toward those in the church, and even sexual intimacy with another. Each of these actions can be profound demonstrations of what it means to promote well-being.

Jesus' own acts of love took many forms and expressions. Rather than being one dimensional, his relational love was full-orbed. Jesus enjoyed fellowship and camaraderie in love with disciples and others, for instance. He loved children and helped those in need. He loved strangers and those who considered themselves his enemies. In fact, Jesus gave his life for others. In all these ways and more, Jesus reveals that God's love is full-orbed.

The relationality of love proves especially important in God's call to love in particular ways. In moment-by-moment living, the loving thing we should do often depends on the context. When others hurt us, for instance, God often calls us to express *agape* that repays evil with good. When we find others suffering, God often calls us to express compassion and acts of service. God sometimes calls us to be a friend to the friendless. Other times, we are called to appreciate the beauty and goodness of God's creation in loving adoration of its Creator. In these instances and others, the relations we have influence the kinds of love God call us to express.

Conclusion

It is little wonder Christians are attracted to relational theology. So long as they keep Scripture at the heart of how they understand God, the themes of love and the relations that love requires will continue to play a primary role in Christian life and doctrine. Relational theology remains central, because love is central to Christian living and thinking.

The Image of God
Samuel M. Powell

"Then God said, 'Let us make humankind in our image, according to our likeness; and let them have dominion over the fish of the sea, and over the birds of the air, and over the cattle, and over all the wild animals of the earth, and over every creeping thing that creeps upon the earth'. So God created humankind in his image, in the image of God he created them; male and female he created them" (Gen 1:26–27).

Because we are created in the image of God, our existence is marked by relationships. To be the creaturely image of God is to be essentially and unavoidably related to God, to fellow humans, and to the rest of creation.

Genesis tells us that we are made in God's likeness. Of course, this doesn't mean that we resemble God physically. But we are like God in other ways. John Wesley thought of the image of God in a three-fold way: (1) we share in God's lordship or dominion (the political image);(2) like God, we are rational beings, possessing intellect and will (the natural image); and (3) we share in God's holiness (the moral image).

Genesis is telling us that who we are—our most fundamental nature—is determined by God's creative act, and in this act something of God passes over into human nature. But it tells us also that in creating human beings, God makes creatures responsible to God. We must answer to God for the use of the dominion we have received. We should use our intellect and will in ways that honor the God whom they reflect. We are to be holy as God is holy. Our resemblance to God thus establishes a moral demand; our relation to God is a relation not only of likeness but also of responsibility.

Because we are created in the image of God, we stand in moral relationships to each other. Just as our status creates a moral relationship to God, so it establishes a moral relation to fellow humans. As Genesis teaches, "Whoever sheds the blood of a human, by a human shall that person's blood be shed; for in his own image God made humankind" (Gen 9:6). The fact that we are images of God grants to human beings a protected status; unjust killing of a fellow human is forbidden precisely because we reflect God. We must refrain from injustice because we are images of the God who is just.

The moral obligation resting on us as the image of God goes beyond unjust killing. Because we are created in God's image, each of us is due the highest moral consideration in every respect. That's why the Letter of James notes, "With [our speech] we bless the Lord and Father, and with it we curse those who are made in the likeness of God" (Jas 3:9). It is saying that there is something deeply wrong with speaking ill of those who reflect God. To be created in God's image is to be a member of a human community in which everyone should receive respect, dignity, and consideration. The image of God thus conditions the moral relationships between one human and another.

What John Wesley called the political image—the dominion that God has given us in the created world—establishes a relationship between human beings and the rest of creation. We are to "have dominion" over other creatures. Historically, Christians have taken this to mean that we are the earth's rulers, and the world exists for us and our benefit. Until recently, this interpretation posed no problems. The small number of humans meant that our use of natural resources was sustainable.

Today, however, the dramatic increase in population and the increasing level of consumption means that dominion should no longer be thought of strictly in terms of rule and use. Instead of thinking of dominion as license to use and consume, we should think of it as the New Testament does. In the kingdom of God, greatness is measured not by the exercise of power and rights. It is measured by humility and servanthood. Today, we should think of dominion in terms of giving as well as using.

The New Testament's greatest contribution to our understanding of God's image is the way it identifies that image with Jesus Christ, "the image of the invisible God" (Col 1:15). While we are truly images of

God, for a full and complete picture of God's image, we must look to Jesus. We are creaturely and frail images of the one and true image.

The New Testament also helps us see that being created in God's image is not so much a status as it is a project, a task of moving toward a goal by the process of sanctification. As the New Testament says, we are to be renewed according to the image of God (Col 3:10). We "are being transformed" into the image (2 Cor 3:18). We are to be conformed to the image that is Jesus (Rom 8:29). And we are destined to bear the image of the heavenly man (1 Cor 15:49).

All these passages interpret our being God's image in terms of transformation and movement. So although it is our created nature to be the image of God, that created nature is not complete. Instead, it is a project for us to undertake, the project of becoming like Jesus through the life of sanctification.

Because being the image of God is a project, it is something that we must learn. We learn what it means to be God's image by imitating Jesus, who is the true image of God. When we look to Jesus, we learn (1) what it means to be a likeness of God and to be morally responsible to God, (2) how we should relate to our fellow humans who bear the image of God, (3) and how we should practice dominion and relate to other creatures.

The Freedom Inherent in Relational Theology

Brint Montgomery

In this essay, I consider two ways of viewing free will. Both are relevant to a relational view of God, and most in the Christian faith have adopted one or the other. The first view of free will, called "compatibilist free will," is the ability to do what you want to do. The second view of free will, "libertarian free will," is the ability to do what you want to do and *the* ability to do otherwise than you did.

Admittedly, free will is a concept difficult to pin down. People's intuitions vary about what makes them free. Consequently, there are many opinions on the matter. Generally, we want people to be morally responsible for their actions. If they are truly responsible, they must be the "actors" in question.

Of course, people don't always agree about the concept of responsibility. Many wonder when one performs a morally "good" act. Given a system where God is the reference standard for all morality, when are one's act correctly assessed as "sin?"

Part of what's at issue is our asking what makes humans unique compared to other animals. We say that humans are at least partially in control of their actions. But when we observe the behaviors of animals, they too seem at least partially in control of their actions.

In addition, we want the notion of "control" to be more than just being the bodily origin of behaviors. We want control to be based on our own choice, where our minds originate the behaviors—not just our genes or environment.

Even more worrisome than distinguishing our control of action from animals' is the idea of self. We don't want to be a mere extension of God, for then the idea of a self disappears. Any notion of moral responsibility seems to disappear if there is no self that is distinguishable from God.

Consider the analogy of a hand. A hand has no free will. It makes no choices, and it has no reflective awareness of a self. Its behaviors are merely an extension of prior decisions and acts. How odd it would be to say in court: "Your honor, I didn't murder that man. My hand did it!" It would be equally strange to say, "I didn't drive my car to work this morning. God did it!" The Department of Motor Vehicles is right not to issue driver's licenses to people who make such claims.

If a hand *never* has free will, we might wonder if we have free will. But if there are *no* times we have free will, how could we talk of being morally responsible for our actions? We couldn't. We have to be in control of our will, but in a unique way.

Many people think God determines everything that happens. A tornado, earthquake, sickness, or (seeming) accidents are all, they say, just God pulling the strings of the system. Yet it's natural to worry along these lines: "if God is doing everything, how could I or anyone possibly have a free will?"

Within the Christian tradition, some people have held that God could be controlling everything and while humans yet remain free. If someone thinks free will is compatible with determinism, that person is called, not surprisingly, a "compatibilist."

But just what kind of free will would one have if God is controlling everything, either directly as we control a hand or indirectly by designing the laws of nature to operate a certain way? Compatibilists answer this by saying that persons are free if they are simply doing what they *want* to do. But I think this answer is mistaken.

Let me illustrate the problem of saying that persons are free if they do what they *want*, even though entirely controlled by God or other forces. There are people who are both pharmacologically and psychologically addicted to drugs. Not only do their bodies crave drugs, their wills continually focus on obtaining the singular thing so damaging to them. Given the state of their wills, we say they "want" the drugs. As they act to get the drugs, they are doing what they "want" to do.

The problem is it doesn't seem that these addicts can do otherwise. Wait long enough, and their wants will indeed drive them. But what's driving them is not a choice but the effects of addiction.

We often hear someone say something like, "My wanting it overpowered me!" But we don't hear people say, "My choosing it overpowered me!" So there is an important conceptual difference between "wanting" to do something and "choosing" it. Merely saying that having a free will is doing what we want is inadequate.

There is another, more satisfactory view of free will far more productive for assessing how people talk about choosing and acting. Being free is not *just* doing what you want to do. It is also being able to have done *otherwise* than you did.

Suppose you were in jail and actually wanted to be there. If the door were opened, the jailer was your friend, or there were no locks or impediments between you and the exit, etc., you could simply walk out of the jail. But you opt to stay. Whether you change your mind or not, you would have the option of doing otherwise than you did. "You're free to go," as they say.

We can see from such cases that having real options is what matters in terms of free will. Without true freedom, we could not make sense of ethics, or even much of history, for we would be mere extensions of some all-controlling system. That system may be an entirely deterministic natural order or an all-controlling God who moment-by-moment micromanages every event.

A relational account of theology works well only if one can affirm a libertarian view of free will. According to it, God does not determine the course of every action. And God doesn't hold us morally responsible for unchosen effects of actions that couldn't have been otherwise. We are genuinely free to respond well or poorly to God, and we are therefore morally responsible.

Faith in Relations
Wm. Curtis Holtzen

"Faith" is one of those words easy to use but difficult to define. Some Christians understand faith as affirming a set of beliefs about God and Christ. Others see faith more in terms of trust in God. Some center their faith on a hope related to future events, while others maintain that faith is about serving others and protecting creation here and now. Each of these understandings is right in some way, but none alone captures the essence of faith. Faith includes elements of belief, trust, hope, and practice.

Relationships can be understood in a wide range of terms as well, from more personal relationships like family, marriage, and friends, to casual relationships found between associates, neighbors, and acquaintances. Relationships can be formal, such as in business or between student and teacher. We can even speak about impersonal relationships with things, nature, or ideas. Some relationships are deeply loving with strong commitments, while others are accidental and fleeting. Relationship, like "faith," is a multifaceted notion and not easily defined. When we explore relationship through the notions of love and trust, however, we see that faith and relationship become inseparable.

Faith as Relationship

Relationships, at their best, include love and trust. Relationships between persons who love and trust one another, that is, who intentionally seek the other's best interest and are confident that the other will do the same, are relationships defined by faith. James Fowler says it well: "faith is always *relational*; there is always *another* in faith. 'I trust *in* and am loyal *to ...*" [1] In this sense, relationship and faith are nearly synonymous. A man who is faithful to his wife, a mother who has faith in her child, and a person who faithfully encourages and stands by a friend are all examples of persons in trusting relationships.

Relationships are certainly possible without either love or trust. Business relationships require trust, but love (in the fullest sense, at least) is not necessary. A parent may deeply love a child, but perhaps, because of the child's addictions, the mother can no longer trust her child. I define relationships in which love and trust are fused as "relational faith." Faith in this sense is relationship—relationship at its fullest and most intimate. This is what it means to be faithful to both love and be trustworthy.

God's Faith in Us

For us to "have faith in God" means we are to be in right relationship with God. Faith is to love actively and trust our Father who is the author of all good gifts (Ja 1:17). We love God by seeking to do what God desires for our lives, that is, what pleases God. Likewise we trust God by living in obedience to Christ's teachings and learning to see the world as God sees it. Our relationship with God is the same as our faith in God—lived out and expressed in love and trust.

I like the way F. Gerrit Immink puts it: "Faith is a relationship between subjects, a communal bond between God and humans. A life of faith is not just a matter of taking certain beliefs about God and his salvation to be true; it is also a matter of our trust in God and God's trustworthiness."[2]

If faith is a relationship or communal bond, shouldn't we think of God as someone of faith? From the standpoint of relational theology, the answer is clearly, "Yes!" Faith is relational and relationships are reciprocal, two-sided. Because God is relational, God has faith. God's relationship with us is not only loving but also trusting.

We are quite comfortable speaking about God loving, for we know that God loves the world (Jn 3:16). Likewise, we speak of God as being trustworthy in all things (Ps 22:4-5). But God also seeks to trust us.

---

1   James W. Fowler, *Stages of Faith: The Psychology of Human Development and the Quest for Meaning* (San Francisco: Harper & Row, 1981), 16.

2   F. Gerrit Immink, *Faith: a Practical Theological Reconstruction, Studies in Practical Theology* (Grand Rapids, Mich.: Eerdmans, 2005), 26–27.

Relational theology makes such an assertion plausible. For the relational theologians, human thoughts and actions involve a measure of freedom. We are not wholly compelled by God or nature; we have real freedom to make wise or foolish choices. We are free, because God shares power with creatures. God is not all controlling. God gives us power to enter into right relationship or reject God's plans.

In concert with the idea of human freedom is the relational idea that God faces an open future. God does not exhaustively know the future for the future does not exist. Freedom is only possible in a world in which the future is unwritten. If humans are free and the future open, God must relate to us in faith, not in absolute certainty. God loves us and has plans for the church. Because of the freedom God has given and because we may use that freedom well or poorly, God must trust that we will be faithful.

God's plans seem always to take the form of partnership. The Bible recounts story after story of God commissioning individuals, communities, and nations for various duties. These partnerships are spoken of in terms of covenants between God and Noah, Abraham, or Israel. The new covenant brought about with the death, burial, and resurrection of Jesus Christ makes possible yet a new kind of partnership. God invites us to partnership for our good and for the good of all creation.

Where there is faith, however, there is also a measure of risk. God's faith is not immune to frustration and heartbreak. Just as we experience the pain and sorrow of infidelity and broken trust, God too feels such pains. God knows we are fallible, but God is willing to take a risk and enter into relationship with us. Empowered by God, we can show ourselves trustworthy and faithful. God's love is unconditional and everlasting, but we must prove ourselves faithful.[3] Just as God tested Abraham to see if he was trustworthy, God seeks for us to show our faithfulness in response to God.

To have faith in God is to be in right relationship with God. It is to love and trust who God is. Likewise, for God to be in relationship with us means that God loves us and trusts us to be a faithful partner in the divine mission for the world. A relational God is a God of faith.

3　　The idea of proving ourselves trustworthy is the theme of Jesus' discourse in Matthew 24 and his parables of the Ten Virgins and the Talents found in chapter 25.

Sin in Relational Perspective

Michael Lodahl

The gospels repeatedly describe Jesus Christ as summarizing the Laws of Moses under the two great commandments: loving God with all of our being (Deut 6:4–6) and loving our neighbors as we love ourselves (Lev 19:18). Accordingly, a relational interpretation of the Christian faith proceeds on the assumption that God has created us human beings to *be loved* and to *love*. In the light of this crucial teaching of Jesus, I suggest as a beginning point for hamartiology (the doctrine of sin) that *sin* is a term that may be identified with any falling short of God's ideal for us: a life of love.

We may be tempted simply to think of love and sin in moralistic terms—that you and I choose our everyday behaviors, and it is up to us to decide, in each moment of our lives, whether we will live in a loving way toward God and other people. There is undoubtedly some truth in this. When we think along these lines, we might find John Wesley's famous definition of sin to be helpful: "a willful transgression of a known law of God." With this definition, Wesley was trying to avoid the idea that we all "sin every day in word, thought and deed." He denied that sinning is an inevitable and constant aspect of every human life.

Wesley's careful definition includes the important adjectives "willful" and "known," both of which contribute importantly to a relational understanding of sin. The term "willful" implies that my real sense of choice is involved, that I am not simply the victim of forces beyond my knowledge or control. The term "known" implies that I am aware of what I am doing, and that I am intentionally and consciously rejecting what I believe to be God's will for me and choosing to pursue some other path.

Particularly when we appreciate the extent to which Wesley identified the law of God with love—he happily cited Paul's words, "whoever loves another has fulfilled the law," for "love is the fulfilling of the law" (Rom 13:8, 10)—we can understand sin as the intentional rejection on our part, at any given moment, of God's calling upon us to live lives of love.

This dimension of the doctrine of sin should not be overlooked or downplayed. We recall Jesus teaching his disciples that just as God loves all people—the evil and the good, the righteous and the unrighteous—so also we are to love our enemies. It is in this context that Jesus calls us to "be perfect, therefore, as your heavenly Father is perfect" (Mt 5:43–48).

The Greek term translated here into English as "perfect" is *teleios*, an adjective derived from *telos*—goal, purpose, aim. The "perfection" or purpose highlighted by Jesus in the Sermon on the Mount is a Godlike love for all people. We should assume that Jesus really does mean this, and that when we fail to love others, including strangers (Mt 5:46–47; cf. Lev 19:33–34) and even so-called "enemies," we are falling short of the "perfection" to which Jesus calls his followers.

Real choices in everyday situations are demanded in this call to love others as God loves all. If the "known law of God" is most fundamentally love for others, then sin is, at root, any willful or intentional transgression against this law of love in our concrete dealings with others. To repeat: this interpretation of sin has its place, an important place. But it is not the whole story.

A relational understanding of sin must also carefully consider how deeply we human beings are interconnected with one another, not to mention with all other creatures (living and non-living) in the world. This notion of human solidarity implies that no one exists "on one's own." Therefore, no one sins "on one's own."

The power of the symbolism of the Hebrew term *adam* as "earthling" is that it underscores our solidarity with all of humanity and with all other earthly creatures. It does not suggest that each of us is our own Adam, our own Eve. It is much more that we are all, throughout human history, Adam and Eve together. Our temptations, our choices, our moral fiber, our weakened sense of God are inseparably intertwined with all other human beings. We are intertwined not only with the millions who share our planet today, but with all who have preceded us and all who will follow us.

Violence today will call forth retaliation tomorrow, and so on, in the cycle of hurt, grief, and pain. For instance, the practice in previous centuries of white Europeans and North Americans enslaving African people continues to reverberate in our times with deep-seated racial fears, mistrust, suspicion, and anger. We know that an addicted woman today may give birth to a crack-cocaine baby tomorrow—and we should appreciate, as well, that the mother's addiction is intertwined with historical, social, and political cycles that are far larger and more comprehensive than a woman's individual choice. "Just Say No" is a profoundly inadequate solution to the power of sin in the world. This is truth about human interconnectedness that St. Augustine reckoned well.

Nonetheless, Augustine's theological opponent Pelagius was in a sense also correct. The opening chapters of Genesis, and the testimony of Scripture as a whole, teach us that each of us stands before God as a responsible actor. God interrogates us, making us answerable for our lives by asking those Genesis questions "Where are you" and "Where is your brother?" (3:9, 4:9).

The good news is that, as Paul proclaims in Romans, God in response to the universality of human sin "gave up [his own Son] for all of us" such that "Jesus our Lord ... was handed over to death for our trespasses and was raised for our justification" (Rom 8:32, 4:25). In the midst of countless relations that influence us in ways we know and others that we cannot fathom, God in Christ makes possible a life free from an orientation toward sin and empowers us to live relationally in love.

A Relational Understanding of Atonement

Derek Flood

Relationships are at the core of who we are. They are the source of our most profound joy and pain. In relationship, we find out who we are as humans and what matters most in life.

Throughout Christian history, relationship with God has been the pulse of vibrant faith. We see this in the aching prose of Augustine's *Confessions*, the wounded and intimate visions of Julian of Norwich's *Revelations of Divine Love*, and the stirring chords of John Newton's classic hymn *Amazing Grace*. Relationships are so central to who we are and to Scripture that one can hardly think of a more fertile soil for theological reflection.

Relationship is the primary lens through which we must understand atonement—the work of God for the salvation of humanity. The story of God's initiative to bring us into loving relationship is the master narratives of Scripture, the main plotline in God's theo-drama.

In saying this, we should not limit ourselves to relational *language* when speaking of the atonement. Scripture enlists a wide array of colorful metaphors and imagery. At the heart of this multifaceted language about God, however, lies the foundational guiding narrative of relationship. In atonement, God acts first to reconcile the relationship we have estranged. Through Jesus' life, death, and resurrection, we are invited to respond to God's invitation for reconciliation. In other words, the atonement is primarily about Christ's work to restore us into a loving relationship with God.

The atonement is above all a demonstration of God's love. We find this point repeatedly throughout the history of the church. It may even seem self-evident. We can easily lose this point, however, in the technical jargon surrounding atonement theology. It can be drowned out by the focus on a legal understanding of the atonement, which speaks of the "demands of justice" for punishment and the need for "satisfaction" and "appeasement."

It's critical to keep in mind the relational focus of the cross for atonement: The cross of Christ is primarily about *love*. Jesus tells his disciples, "Greater love has no one than this: to lay down one's life for one's friends" (Jn 15:13). Paul amplifies this by saying God loved us in this way "while we were yet sinners." Christ died for us while we were "God's enemies" (Rom 5:8–10).

The cross demonstrates God's enemy love. It is not the condition for God's love or forgiveness. That condition is God. God in love initiated the atonement; God "first loved us" (1 Jn 4:19). God does not need to be reconciled. We do!

A relational understanding also gives insight into how the atonement makes possible our salvation. Paul speaks frequently of Christ dying "for us." This certainly means that Christ died *for our sake*. But some scholars argue Paul does not describe "for us" in terms of substitution—that is, in terms of Christ dying *instead of* us or *in our place*. Instead, Paul speaks of our dying "with Christ" so we can also rise with him. Here the vicarious nature of both the death and resurrection of Christ is framed in the relational terms of participation and union.

Perhaps the most powerful expression of this is Paul's statement that Jesus was "made to be sin for us, so that we might become the righteousness of God in him" (2 Cor 5:21). Christ was *made* into sin, so that we would be *made* into God's righteousness.

This is an astounding statment, but how does this take place? Again, we see a relational connection: Christ died *for us* so we could live *in him* and *with him*. Through intimate union with God in Christ in a living personal relationship, we are transformed into his likeness. We do not merely follow his example. Rather, we become Christlike through *abiding* in Christ, through living in God. Here the vicarious nature of the atonement takes on the most intimate and relational terms, language we find echoed in Paul's analogies of adoption and marriage union.

Paul writes that our experience of a loving relationship with God here and now acts as the "first fruits." This first fruit is the divine deposit pointing to our future hope of eternal life. This relationship is the ground for our hope for the ultimate end of sickness, death, and injustice—not just for us, but for all of creation (2 Cor 5:5). The scope of salvation that New Testament writers envision, while being deeply personal, is not limited to individual salvation.

Salvation is also not focused solely on personal guilt. While some people struggle with guilt, many feel separated from God by what was done to them. They feel victimized. This may take the form of devastating brokenness resulting from abusive relationships. Or it may come from personal tragedy or injustice. For instance, a friend of mine told me through tears that she had stopped believing in God at the age of fourteen when her father died of cancer. Sin, sickness, and suffering can all cause us to become alienated from God. The cross overcomes these barriers.

The cross reveals the crucified God's solidarity with us in our pain, lostness, and darkness. In the incarnation, God in Christ entered our wretched, broken, sinful estate—into the depth of our disease. This is what Jürgen Moltmann calls "the crucified God," an image that undoes theologies of triumphalism.

This image of the suffering God revealed in the weakness of the cross means that no matter how helpless and alone we may feel, God is with us. When we see God so transparent and open—stripped naked on a cross—we realize we can be real, transparent, and unafraid. When we are honest, we know we have needs and dark places in our lives. God meets us there unmasked.

Once again, we see the relational connection: God stooping to us in love, meeting us at the point of our need. Evil and death do not overcome the God who is vulnerable and close. Rather, Jesus' way of enemy love overcomes the world. In Christ, we have hope in the midst of darkness. In Christ's atoning work, we can be be reconciled into a loving relationship with God. Living in that relationship and walking in the way of Jesus, we become ministers of that reconciliation.

A Relational View of Salvation and Sanctification

Timothy J. Crutcher

When they think about salvation, many Christians immediately think of heaven. In fact, most Christians would probably say that "being saved" and "going to heaven" mean the same thing. While the hope of heaven is a very important feature of the Christian life and the Kingdom of God, a relational approach to the question of salvation—and its cousin, the question of sanctification—involves much more.

A relational approach to salvation starts with a relational approach to what it is from which we are being saved—sin. Focusing on heaven as the goal of salvation might make us think we need to be saved from this world. But we have to remember God created this world to be good, and this is the place God has put us for now. Unless God made a mistake, this is where we should be.

The world wouldn't be a bad place if we were not constantly twisting it for our own selfish desires. Focusing on ourselves makes it impossible to relate well to others. And our lack of love for others makes it easier for them to be less than loving. The whole thing spirals out into the fallen world as we know it today.

We are most happy and most fulfilled when we are in loving relationships. That's what we were made for. And that's what the self-focus that we call sin destroys. In fact, you might even say the sin we need to be saved from is anything that disrupts or violates our loving relationships with God and other people.

When we act in self-centered ways and make ourselves more important that those around us, we hurt the relationships we have with others. That puts barriers between others and us, and it isolates us from them.

Although we create those barriers, once they are "out there," they are out of our control. We know if we have offended someone, we might not be able to fix that broken relationship simply by saying "I'm sorry." The "guilt"—and that's a good word for it—we create needs to be forgiven by those we offend before the relationship can be restored. So, ironically, focusing on ourselves breaks relationships. But focusing on others helps to repair them.

Essentially, that's what's going on in salvation. By our selfish behavior, we have messed up our primary relationship—our relationship to God. Because of that, we have messed up the other relationships in our lives as well.

God, through the work of Christ, has made provision for fixing that relationship. Through the convicting power of the Holy Spirit, God lets us see the mess we've made. We realize our guilt and accept God's offer of forgiveness. This restores our relationship to God and sets the stage by which we can begin to redeem and even deepen the relationships we have with everyone else.

Sin is really about broken relationships more than anything else. Salvation is salvation from sin. Salvation is really about God empowering us to repair those broken relationships. This brings us back into fellowship with God and enables us to live in right relationship with everyone else.

This is what Jesus was referring to when asked what the greatest commandment was. Love God, he said, but also love your neighbor. That's pretty much the whole shooting match as far as Jesus was concerned. Everything else is details.

Of course, even when we have been brought back into right relationship with God, we still find ourselves with a problem. We are still the same kind of people with the same kind of selfish desires that messed up that relationship in the first place. And those selfish desires continually invite us to choose for ourselves instead of those we are called to love.

Our relational problem is deeper than the fact we have broken our relationships and need forgiveness. We are the kind of people who still wrestle with our self-centered nature in ways that make it easy to keep breaking relationships.

Some Christian traditions say that that is just the way it is. That's the Christian life, a life of constantly wrestling with selfishness and asking forgiveness when we fail. While there is probably always some sense of struggle involved in becoming all God wants us to become, it would be depressing if we felt ourselves doomed always to the same struggle.

That's why we need sanctification. In our personal relationships, we grow together in ways that make those relationships easier and easier to prioritize. We often don't think twice about sacrificing for a friend, where we might have to consider seriously the same sacrifice for a stranger.

So, too, in our relationship with God, God empowers us by grace to become more like God. Our relationship with God becomes more "natural." We also relate to other people more like God relates to them—in unconditional, self-giving love—as we grow with God and with them.

Like salvation, this growth happens both in sudden and gradual ways. We have moments of deep crisis and reorientation of our life. But we also have those gradual movements of relationally deepening as we practice the love we have come to know through God's grace.

Looking at salvation and sanctification through a relational lens does nothing to diminish the hope that we have of one day living in a place—heaven—where all of our relationships are all that they can be. But it helps us to focus on the here-and-now aspects of God's work in our lives. God enables us to live in right relationship with God now. God uses that relationship to empower the way we relate to others in everyday life.

II.
Biblical Witness in
Relational Perspective

Cooperative Covenant Partners in the Bible

Karen Strand Winslow

The stories in the Bible show that God's plans were activated when people became cooperative covenant partners.[1] God relied on them to accomplish tasks that produced and preserved a people through whom salvation could come to the world. In fact, it's hard to find a story in which the characters do not affect the plot, a plot that God set in motion, to be sure.

The voluntary obedience of Abraham, Jacob, Joseph, Moses, Isaiah, Jeremiah, and Mary was necessary to the divine enterprise of bringing God's perspectives, promises, and provision. The desperate ingenuity of Sarah, Rebekah, Rachel, Leah, Tamar, Zipporah, Rahab, Ruth, Hannah, Bathsheba, and other women was also necessary. These characters used their wits, desperation, wisdom, position, faith confessions, and urgent prayers to shape Israel's unfolding story.

Jesus was God's unique covenant partner. His obedience unto death led to the reconciliation of the world to God. Jesus said, "not my will but your will be done." Although this is the quintessential sacrifice, Jesus followed and preceded other friends of God who said: "speak, Lord, for your servant hears" (Samuel) or "here I am; send me" (Isaiah) or "let it be unto me according to your word" (Mary) or rose early in the morning and took his son Isaac three days journey to the place God would show him. Many others also walked after God, obeying with their feet (all of Jesus' followers).

---

1   This is a term I first heard from a former colleague, Dr. Dwight (Rip) Van Winkle of Seattle Pacific University.

49

A close reading of any of the biblical stories demonstrates that what God's partners said and did influenced the outcome of a plan God initiated. Some of the stories indicate Israel was preserved when a determined person—usually a woman—used unusual means to protect life, whether her own or others. For example, Tamar and Hannah were desperate for children. Tamar pretended to be a prostitute in order to become pregnant by Judah and thus the tribe of Judah was produced. Zipporah saved Moses' life by circumcising her son and thus Moses was able to go back to Egypt to pull the Lord's people out of their situation. Hannah prayed with anguish for a son she could lend back to the Lord, Samuel, who brought the word of the Lord to Israel as judge, prophet, priest, and kingmaker.

Since God's plans are about and for people, God regularly relies on people to bring those plans to pass. Even the stories telling how people resisted show the importance of cooperation. Saul, David, and Solomon all pleased God when they humbly relied on him. They disappointed God after they had grown powerful and paranoid, lazy and lustful, or were ensnared by other gods. When kings honored their relationship with God, they helped create a nation with whom God could dwell and through whom God could bless the entire world. When they broke covenant, they wreaked havoc for their people who were eventually expelled from the land, but never from God's loving presence (2 Kings 25, Jeremiah).

Moses epitomizes the uneven yet poignant ways that biblical characters cooperated with God. God's reliance upon Moses was demonstrated from their first meeting and it continued throughout their complicated partnership. When God heard the cries of Israelite slaves, God said to Moses "I will send *you*" (Ex 3–4). Moses did not immediately say: "I'll go where you want me to go, dear Lord." But God did not give up. After God responded to Moses' excuses by allowing Aaron to be his spokesman, Moses left for Egypt. Although Moses verbally refused to go multiple times, he obeyed with his feet. He confronted Pharaoh and led the people out of Egypt and into a covenant relationship with God (Ex 19–32, especially Ex 24).

Moses became God's most intimate conversation partner (Ex 32–34, Num 12, Deut 34:10–12). Moses challenged God many times as one friend would confront another. The first time was over Pharaoh's harsh reaction to Moses' request to let the people leave for a few days. But God reassured him (Ex 5:22). Later, when God exploded in anger over Aaron's golden calf and Israel's apostasy and rebellions, Moses repeatedly urged God to recant from his plan to destroy them and start over. God listened (Ex 32; Num 13–14). Although God was thoroughly disappointed and disgusted with Israel (the text says his "nose grew hot"), God restrained from slaying them because of Moses' reasoning *and* their relationship. God punished Israel and refused to allow the faithless generation to enter the land. Although God could barely tolerate immature apostasy at the outset of their relationship, Israel experienced God's faithfulness over the long term.

Israel was supposed to remain God's intimate, covenant people. After all, Moses was God's intimate, covenant partner. Israel had "married" God in Exod 24, saying "I will" in a ceremony much like a wedding. And yet they so quickly forgot the God with whom they were bonded ("I, Yahweh, your God, am a jealous God" [Ex 20:5]).

Moses' "nose grew hot" as well. He was prohibited from entering the land because of his reaction to the whining people (Num 20:1–13). Yes, he was friends with God. Yes, there was no prophet like Moses who saw God face to face and spoke with him mouth to mouth (Ex 33:11, Num 12:7–8, Deut 34:10–12). And, yes, God used Moses to function as a mouthpiece for him and to mediate the covenant. But Moses was required to set God apart as holy before the people and follow God's instructions closely. The kings of Israel—and all of us—must learn from Moses' severe sentence. To be partners with God, we must closely respect that relationship by submitting to the words and salvific acts of the LORD (1 Sam 12; 1 Kings 13–14; 21–22, Jn 13–17).

Moses' story is not unique in showing how God relies on relationship with covenant partners. Biblical characters often affect the plot God set in motion. These inventive people not only add color, flavor, and texture to the stories. They shaped the story itself. And so do we.

The Authority of the Bible
Dwight Swanson

The phrase "the authority of the Bible" essentially means that the Bible, comprising the Old and New Testaments, is the basis and source for Christians for understanding God's revelation to humanity. This revelation is found definitively in the incarnation of Jesus Christ. Beyond this, less common ground exists among the various and sundry branches of Christianity. A primary area of divergence is on the question whether this authority is intrinsic to the Scriptures or extrinsic, requiring acknowledgment as authoritative by past and present communities of faith.

Appeal to intrinsic authority—that is, that which comes from within Scripture—is made by reference to inspiration. Traditional theologies will cite the witness of Scripture itself to its divine origin. The Lord commands Moses, for instance. The word of the Lord comes to the prophets through visions and oracles. And, particularly, 2 Timothy 3:16: "All scripture is inspired by God and is useful for teaching, for reproof, for correction, and for training in righteousness." This begs the question of what "all scripture" means, or what it means to be "inspired."

Authority is also understood by reference to the canon and its development through communities consisting of individuals in relationship to one another and to the text. This takes into account the manner in which the particular books that comprise the Bible came to be accepted as Scripture. For the earliest Christians "the Bible" was what we call the Old Testament. But no single Christian congregation would have copies of all the books to read. And the selection of what was considered Scripture varied widely from what we now find between the covers of a single book.

As for the New Testament, the earliest copies bound in a single codex—from the 4th century—each include books not found in modern Bibles. In fact, modern English Bibles used by Evangelical Christians are based on decisions regarding the canon made during the 16th century Reformation. This highlights the extrinsic nature of the authority of the Bible. Protestants differ from Roman Catholics and Orthodox Christianity in this way. As such, emphasis is placed on communities of faith as arbiters of what is authoritative as Scripture.

Bound up with belief in the authority of the Bible is the matter of authoritative interpretation of Scripture. The 400th anniversary of the publication of the King James Version of the Bible in 2011 draws attention to the impact William Tyndale has had on English Christianity. Tyndale's translation of the Bible into English lies behind most of today's versions. It was an act of defiance against church authority, particularly that of the Pope, that led to this translation. The famous line: "I will cause the boy that driveth the plough to know more of the Scriptures than thou dost!" was a cry against the Church's monopoly on not only the interpretation of, but also access to, Scripture.

Whatever may be made of Tyndale's intent, the result in 21st century Evangelicalism is that authority of interpretation does not lie with the teachers, but with every reader. Every Bible study may go around the circle of devoted students and ask, "What does this mean to you?" Each person may express his or her understanding, and—in the end—all are equally valid. Equally, a man trained in mechanical engineering can find the date of the return of Christ through his own study of the Bible. He can spend millions advertising his interpretation, and millions will believe simply because he says the Bible says so. Authoritative interpretation is wholly individualized.

This says nothing, of course, of the authority of the Bible itself. Evangelicals affirm that the Bible is the authoritative word of God, usually adding that this authority is higher than "human tradition." This means that any interpretation of Scripture that comes from the Church is human, while true interpretation comes directly to each believer without any such mediation.

It is not too difficult to see the fallacy of this viewpoint, when expressed in this manner. No person comes to the Bible without being taught, in one way or another, what to expect. Even the "no human tradition" viewpoint is a human tradition. The assumption that the Bible may be taken literally, or that it is true with regard not only to matters of faith but also of science, history, and geography are modern traditions about authoritative interpretation of Scripture. It is fair, then, to ask why these "human traditions" should be considered more valid than those tracing their roots through centuries of wrestling with revelation.

The Bible is the authority to which Christians look for understanding what it means to be Christian, to be the people of God, and of what God's purposes for his creation are. The idea that these books, and not others, determine Christian faith came about through the crucible of early Christian experience and conflict of understanding. The community of faith, together, came to say that in these books we recognize God's revelation. Others may be useful and commendable, but they are not a part of this revelation.

Out of this common ground came the important questions of how to understand this revelation, and what understandings can be Christian or not. Nearly two thousand years of historical debate and theology show this to be a constant and unending task. Authoritative interpretation does not lie with church authorities; nor does it lie with the individual alone. Nor is it only the domain of the scholars of Scripture. Authority lies with the Church—of which all of these are part.

This means interpretation, to be genuine, will be a constant conversation within the Church. This includes the local manifestation of the Church, where pastors, teachers, and laity engage the issues of life and death in conversation with Scripture. Scholars engage with Church leaders and parishioners. This conversation cannot stay within denominational boundaries, but occurs among theological and confessional traditions.

All of this presupposes a relational understanding of what comprises good biblical interpretation. Pastors, scholars, laity, leaders, traditions, and others listen to and influence one another in ongoing relationships and in relation with the Holy Spirit. The Bible is authoritative, then, as the ground from which the Church engages the ongoing interpretive task of communicating the gospel of Jesus Christ to God's world.

The Revelation and Inspiration of Scripture

Dennis Bratcher

The concept of revelation lies at the heart of Christian faith. Christians believe God is uniquely revealed to humanity in human history. Christianity is a response to God's self-disclosure. Augustine and some others in the early church understood *all* knowledge as revealed by God. This idea made its way into various forms of modern thinking, usually through traditions that use the sovereignty of God as a primary theological category. Some adopt this view in relation to the Bible and believe it covers all knowledge and data. In their view, Scripture is seen in absolute categories, and they often use the terms *inerrant* and *infallible* to describe Scripture.

I do not view Scripture in those terms. Instead, Scripture is the witness that the community of faith has borne to or about revelation. In other words, *God* is the content of the revelation. Scripture tells us about and points toward that revelation. Scripture is revelatory in the secondary sense, because it is a witness and response to God's own revelation. God revealed Himself in history (events), and the community of faith interpreted those events in what we now have as Scripture. The Scriptures reflect this dynamic of the "story of God" woven into the life of the community of faith through the centuries.

This suggests that the people who told the story influenced the way the story of God emerged. And it suggests that how people hear the story will influence their understanding of it. While we affirm that the testimony is true, the vehicle of the testimony was conditioned by the culture, language, knowledge (or lack of it), historical experience, personality, ethos, etc., of the people who passed on the testimony. And it was influenced by those who grappled with the implications of the story as the people of God.

We also hear the story of God in culturally conditioned ways. We bring our own culture, language, knowledge (or lack of it), historical experience, personality, ethos, etc., to the biblical text. We grapple with its implications in living out what it means to be people of God.

Despite these conditions, the Bible remains revelatory to us today. This does not mean Scripture is absolute, final, and therefore the truth about everything. That is the position of Fundamentalism, literalism, and inerrancy. These positions are actually a fairly recent development in Christian history.

Instead, Scripture is revelatory in the precise sense that God reveals Himself in history in the dynamic of the community as they bear witness to "what we have seen and heard" (Acts 4:20). Scripture is living and active. God continues to confront people in their own history.

This brings us to the importance of affirming God's role in shaping Scripture. Here is where a relational concept of inspiration of Scripture provides some help.

There are many theories of inspiration. The basic issue in inspiration is the balance between God's role and humans' role. On the one pole are dictation and verbal theories affirming that Scripture emerged from God alone, or nearly so. Usually, these are heavily influenced by an absolute sovereignty of God model that allows little human input. This model usually assumes humans are totally contaminated by sin and cannot be trusted.

On the other pole are elevation theories that affirm nearly 100% human authorship. Usually, these are heavily influenced by models that do not see God active in the world. In the elevation view, Scripture is just a good book reflecting the same kind of elevated human insight that, for example, might be found in Shakespeare or *Star Wars*.

Between these poles are relational theories. Relational theories are usually called "dynamic inspiration," because they try to balance the role of God and humans in a relational way. Any adequate theory of inspiration should be consistent with the larger relational understanding of human beings that arises from Scripture. The Wesleyan tradition calls this perspective "prevenient grace." This is the "going before" grace of God that enables humans to respond to God.

Let me explain how I think the relational process works in the production of Scripture. It all begins with God revealing Himself. With any revelation of God, however, there must be a response from the community or the person. Here is where inspiration comes into play. Not only does God reveal Himself, He helps the people understand that revelation through inspiration. The locus of inspiration tells us about God, about ourselves, and about how we relate to God.

God as Holy Spirit continues to help people understand the message of Scripture long after the original writers put words in print. Relational inspiration is ongoing. It is at work as witnesses tell the story. And it describes how God enables people to hear, understand, and respond to the story.

Exactly *how* humans respond to God's relational inspiration—how they talk about, tell it, theologize about it, pass it on in tradition, incorporate it into ethical and doctrinal systems, etc.,—is influenced by the culture in which they live. They tell the story of God, which God has revealed to them and helped them understand. But they tell it their own ways.

The relational model sees inspiration of Scripture as a process operating within the community of faith rather than a one-time revelation of absolute truth. That is why any reading or study of Scripture should begin with the prayer, "Lord, help us (or me) understand." It is an acknowledgment of that relational quality of inspiration, and it confesses that God makes Scripture come alive!

The relational model fits the Wesleyan perspective of the balance between God's grace and human freedom. God can entrust people with the testimony to divine grace as He continually works with them individually and communally. If He could entrust the Savior of the world to a young Jewish girl from Galilee, surely He can trust to His disciples the testimony to that event. And God can trust this testimony to the resulting community of faith He called into being.

"God with Us": Reading Scripture (Relationally) as the Church

Richard P. Thompson

We often describe God in terms of love—a description that is relational in nature. We see God's loving action in the ways God initiates relationship with the humans God creates. Among the first stories in the Bible are those of God's relationship with the first humans God created, Abraham, and the people of Israel. This theme of God's covenant people weaves its way through most books that comprise the Old Testament of the Christian Scriptures. In New Testament books such as the Gospel of Luke and The Acts of the Apostles, the corresponding image of the people of God reappears prominently to show us how God seeks to love, live, and act graciously among all people God redeems.

Although probably all of us affirm this basic understanding of God in terms of love, this seldom affects how Christians read and interpret Scripture. Granted, many persons speak of the Bible as "God's love letter" made available to tell us how much God loves each of us. As helpful as this "love letter" idea may be, however, many see it more in terms of God's love of individuals. They thus move away from this understanding of God's love that seeks relationship with the *people* of God.

In that sense, the *biblical* concept "God is love" has little or no bearing on the way that Christians typically go about reading the Bible. We often hear from well-meaning Christians that we must "return to the Bible." Some even go back to the rallying cry of the Protestant Reformation: "*sola scriptura!*"—"Only Scripture!" In its original 16th century setting, that call sought to affirm the authority of the Christian Scriptures apart from the authority of the Roman Catholic Church.

In contemporary Protestant circles, however, this call has drifted from its original moorings to mean something much different. These calls now focus only on the Bible and its authority for theology. They discount the role or contributions of anything and everything else in the process: other teachings or practices, other Church emphases or contributions, other traditions or ways of thinking. In other words, the suggestion has often come to mean that *nothing* is valid, other than what the Bible *itself* explicitly affirms.

One positive outcome of the Protestant emphasis on Scripture is the proliferation of resources and tools for persons to study the Bible. More than ever, contemporary persons have the ability to study the Scriptures on their own. Individuals can find help in understanding difficult passages and can gain devotional insights not available even a few decades ago.

However, *privatized* reading of the Bible—apart from other Christians and the local worshiping church setting—results in mistaken notions of *sola scriptura* in our day.[1] We have made reading the Bible into an individualistic activity isolated from anybody and everybody else! As a result, we have turned *sola scriptura* into reading Scripture *solo*!

We can see evidence of this isolated-from-others kind of reading. On one hand, there is a lack of accountability to the broader community of faith. It is in the broader context of the Church where the insights, experiences, and skills of the collective community offer something to the reading of Scripture that happens when the Spirit of God guides or inspires readers.[2] This is simply not available to the isolated believer.[3]

---

1   The expression "privatized reading" does not refer to devotional or other readings per se that contribute to the spiritual growth of the individual as long as the individuals live out their faith in tangible ways. The problem with privatized readings is the failure to read and live them out in the context of the Christian faith community.

2   See John Wesley's comment on 2 Tim 3:16 in his *Explanatory Notes upon the New Testament* (London: Epworth, 1958), 794: "The Spirit of God not only once inspired those who wrote it, but continually inspires, supernaturally assists, those that read it with earnest prayer." See Richard P. Thompson, "Inspired Imagination: John Wesley's Concept of Biblical Inspiration and Literary-Critical Studies," in *Reading the Bible in Wesleyan Ways: Some Constructive Proposals*, ed. B. L. Callen and R. P. Thompson (Kansas City, MO: Beacon Hill Press of Kansas City, 2004), 57–79.

3   See Richard P. Thompson, "Community in Conversation: Multiple Readings of Scripture and a Wesleyan Understanding of the Church," in *Reading the*

Wesleyans, who have long affirmed the primacy of Scripture but also the complementary roles of tradition, reason, and experience, declare without hesitation the central place of the Bible as the *Church's* Scriptures.

On the other hand, private readings also tend to ignore the fact that the address of Scripture is not the individual *per se* but the *people* of God. A large percentage of biblical commands are plural rather than singular. The stories focus on God's activity and presence among the people with whom God establishes covenant. There may be good reason, for instance, why the Bible reiterates the need to love one another as often as it does. This reflects the corporate, covenantal, and therefore *relational* context that the biblical texts themselves assume.

The relational nature of both God and Scripture suggests that we reconsider how we think about the task of interpreting Scripture. The purpose behind biblical interpretation is not the rearticulation or explanation of an old set of words and ideas with a set of fresh, updated words. The ultimate goal of interpretation is not gaining information, whether historical or theological, as important as that is.

Rather, the Church appropriated these particular texts as sacred Scripture and continues to interpret them as authoritative Scripture because through them we "heard" and continue to hear God speak to us as God's people. To read Scripture as the Church means that we read with God and with one another. We listen to what God calls of us as the people of God. We also listen to one another, as we discern what that call might mean for us, at this time and in this place.

Even that is not enough. The question remains as to how we respond. The evidence of our interpretation of Scripture may be seen in the ways we go to live and perform faithfully what we have encountered and discovered *together* as the Church through Scripture.

God with *us*. God's presence, activity, and grace among the people of God enable the Bible to become sacred Scripture for the Church. May we listen to God and to one another to discern what God asks of us together as those who are the *ekklēsia* of God, "those who are called by God." For that is what it means to live in relation as the people of God.

Bible in Wesleyan Ways, 179–84.

III.
The Christian Life in Relational Perspective

Relational Theology and Ecclesiology
Philip R. Hamner

O n the day of Pentecost the Spirit of God birthed the church. Suddenly, otherwise weak followers of Jesus Christ were empowered to speak the Good News of the gospel. From that day until now, the church has been intimately linked to its Lord. In fact, it is not overstated to say that there would be no church without this intimate connection. Thus, the place and purpose of ecclesiology—the study of the church—in Christian relational theology is essential. It is in the study of the church that one finds some of the strongest evidence for relational theology.

The Scriptures are filled with images of the interrelationship between the Triune God and the church. A look at a few of these scriptures illustrates this point. In John 17, Jesus demonstrates the deep intimacy that exists between the Father and the Son. The focus of their relationship is in the redemption of creation, specifically the redemption of humanity. Jesus prays first that disciples would know the extent of love shared between Father and Son. Then, Jesus prays that others, who will hear of this love through the witness of the disciples, would know this love is for them.

Such is the heart of God. The love that exists between Father, Son, and Spirit is sent into the world to bring rebellious children into eternal relationship. The very character of God comes alive to restore relationship with a broken and hurting people. God's most profound expression to the world is the very overflow of God's love.

This glorious hope comes with receiving God's grace. As the Apostle Peter says, "His divine power has given us everything needed for life and godliness, through the knowledge of him who called us by his own glory and goodness. Thus he has given us, through these things, his precious and very great promises, so that through them you may escape from the corruption that is in the world because of lust, and *may become participants in the divine nature*" (2 Pet 1:3–4, emphasis added).

The writings of the Apostle Paul reveal another way to see the connection between relational theology and the doctrine of the church. Paul introduces the idea of the church being the body of Christ. In virtually all his writings, Paul makes use of this metaphor in some way, and in several places draws out its implications.

In the Epistle to the Romans, for example, Paul speaks of the dependence members of the body of Christ have on one another. He reminds believers in Rome that such dependence is drawn from the strong connection the church has to its Lord. He writes, "For as in one body we have many members, and not all members have the same function, so we, who are many, are one body in Christ, and individually we are members one of another" (Rom 12:4–5).

In the Epistle to the Ephesians, the Apostle Paul draws a further relational connection between God and the church. When speaking about the love and relationship a husband should have with his wife, he makes the analogy of the church being the Bride of Christ. This intimate reality is given expression and meaning by its connection to the way Christ cared for the church. Paul declares, "Husbands, love your wives, just as Christ loved the church and gave himself for her, in order to make her holy by cleansing her with the washing of water by the word, so as to present the church to himself in splendor, without a spot or wrinkle or anything of the kind—yes, so that she may be holy and without blemish" (Eph 5:25–27).

Elsewhere the Scriptures show us images of relational significance in still one more important way. The apostle Peter takes the ordinary notion of building a house with stones and demonstrates the strong relationships that arise from being connected to the cornerstone. Stones are not likely seen as capable of relationship, but Peter gives his example a unique and important qualifier. He writes, "Come to him, a living stone, though rejected by mortals yet chosen and precious in God's sight, and like living stones, let yourselves be built into a spiritual house, to be a holy priesthood, to offer spiritual sacrifices acceptable to God through Jesus Christ" (1 Pet 2:4–5).

So, it should be clear that the ways in which Scriptures speak about the church have everything to do with relational theology. The examples above demonstrate in different ways the intimate and deep connection between God and church.

At every turn, the Scriptures speak of the church in relational categories. These categories signify the living and active work of God's Spirit to bring life to the church. These relational categories also demonstrate the ongoing way in which God's Spirit provides strength, empowerment, and vitality. It is the movement of God in and through the church that gives it life. It is the absolute need of the church to be in constant communion with its Lord.

Prayer and our Relationship with God
Libby Tedder

Consider playing a word-game for a moment, one where free-association is made with the word "prayer." What comes initially to mind?

Here is a short list of phrases that come immediately to my mind: request, awkward, frustrating, unifying, painful, doubtful, peace, silence, confession, necessary, pointless, worship, grief, joy, needy, glass ceiling, refreshing, vulnerable, comforting, empowering.

When boiled down to its essence, prayer is to relational theology as communication is to relationship. You cannot have one without the other. In fact, prayer is to relationship with God as oxygen is to being alive.

Your reaction to the word "prayer" is probably a mixed bag: a combination of hopeful longing and fear of failure. You may want to deny the unfinished prayer journals or memories when God seemed not to answer your impassioned pleas.

The topic of prayer can be guilt inducing for many Christians. We grasp that prayer is crucial to living like Jesus and building connection with God. But how do we do it, and what does it look like?

Basic communication theory says that messages are delivered through some form or medium. All living creatures communicate, whether by sound, scent, sight, touch, taste or a complex exchange of all senses. Between humans, all interaction has meaning. In the convergence of what we intend and how we interpret, meaning influences all communication.

The same is true of a relationship shared between humans and God. Our words, actions, and postures matter. The reverse is also true; the way God communicates through revelation in creation, scripture, and human stories really matters. There are no unmediated relationships. And without prayer there is no relationship to God!

Prayer is the stuff of relationship with God. I use the very un-precise term "stuff" to mean the context, nature, and effect of how humans and God relate. Without prayer we cannot hope to know God, and limits the way that God communicates with us. The Bible affirms that prayer, as an expression of the God-human relationship, leaves an impression on all participants. The Psalms, for example, record many times that God's people cried for help and God heard and saved them.

Relational theology affirms that prayer affects us. But there is a sense in which it also affects God. And prayer influences what is possible in the present and future. Prayer literally changes the world. The way we relate to God in prayer changes the way we live and move and have our being. By transforming us, prayer transforms the way God is present to the world by opening new ways for love to abound.

How we pray shapes who we are. How we pray influences how God is known on earth. Prayer, as a spiritual activity, is not the same thing as prayers. A favorite author, Barbara Brown Taylor, helps relieve a bit of my guilt-ridden angst about prayer. She says praying is more than saying prayers at set times, in the right places, with the right words. Prayer is waking up to the presence of God.[1]

There are as many ways to pray as there are people. Each moment presents a fresh possibility for interacting with God as unique as the person praying. In prayer, we devote ourselves to cooperating with the God who is on a reconciliation mission. We are most tuned into being alive when we are in the thick of prayer.

The best way to pray is to make it a habit. When my eye catches the twinkling sun filtering through translucent leaves and I become aware of God's resplendent presence in creation, I am in prayer. When my heart is gripped by the injustice of poverty as I greet a homeless sister begging at a street corner, I am in prayer. When together with loved ones we relish the pure laughter of a child, we are in prayer. When my community of faith is moved in obedience to affirm the value of human life by opposing

---

1   Taylor, Barbara Brown. *An Altar in the World: A Geography of Faith* (New York: Harper One. 2009), 178.

nuclear weapons production, we are in prayer. When prayer is habituated, the world is oxygenated with God's love.

Another key component of prayer is honesty. Truthful outcries can be heard from the pages of scripture. God never restricts grace because an emboldened person or community leveled a complaint against evil or mourned in despair (Ps 102, esp. v. 17). Prayers matter, but the point is never to let them get in the way of praying. There is a deep and wide tradition of prayers from which we can draw in Christian tradition, even as we participate in creating new ones.

Prayer can engage all the senses. Praying can be tuning to the inner world of reflections and the outer world electric with clues that God is on the move. Prayer can be paying attention to our inclinations, to our breathing. Taking time to listen to news broadcasts and competing voices blogging on the social media milieu can be prayerful. Holding the wrinkled hand of a grandfather or feeling the thumping rhythms of a nearby car at the traffic light, even there we can be praying as we turn our thoughts to God. Learning how to pray is as much about learning who God is and who we are as it is technique.

Why do we pray? Too many of us function like atheists when it comes to prayer. We claim belief in God, but we do not act on it. From the outside, it looks like our belief is mere lip service to cultural tradition. But prayer is the activating ingredient of faith. Saint Teresa said it well: "[I]t is extraordinary what a difference there is between understanding a thing and knowing it by experience."[2]

When we pray, we make an intentional turn toward God, and we are formed into the Imago Dei. We become more of who we are, knowing more deeply who God is. When we pray, we are aligned with God's love-mission and compelled to live like Jesus. As co-creators with God, we are intimately woven into the fabric of relationship with God and God's saving activity in the world.

We pray, because Jesus taught us to relocate our awareness of who God is and who we are (Mt 6:9–14). We pray, because we need to experience the compassion of our heavenly parent. We pray, because it sharpens our intentions and makes us better listeners. We pray, because it heals us of blind unbelief and opens our eyes to God's will on earth. We pray, because we are never actually alone in this world. We pray, because

2   Saint Teresa of Avila, "The Life of St. Teresa of Jesus" (Chap. 13, ¶ 13) http://www.jesus-passion.com/life_of_st_teresa_of_jesus_Part2.htm >

we remember our true dependence when naming our daily needs: bread, forgiveness, peace with neighbors, and protection from trial. We pray, because we need help to see where the leavening yeast of God's grace is being kneaded into every nook and cranny of creation. We pray, so that when God's redemption is baked into our lives and begins to rise throughout the world, we can share it with the hungry.

If we are not practicing the hospitable discipline of prayer, God's love does not dwell deep within us, and our relational capacity is diminished. There must be room for all who thirst for living water to join us at the well that will never dry. If we are not praying we are malnourished without the ears to hear or eyes to see. We pray to usher in God's kingdom—here and now.

What if we feel as though God does not respond? It may be impossible to talk about unanswered prayer without sounding naïve or calloused. Our petitions are only a sliver of the whole experience of prayer, but I'd be remiss not to talk about God seeming unresponsive. Discerning answers to prayer can only be confirmed in the Spirit-breathed artistry of our own lives, and through the communal affirmation of the Church. God's answers come in the form of our interconnected, on-going passions and yearnings within the community of faith.

Some prayers will go unanswered, as far as we can tell. This does not mean we should quit expressing our strongest desires or deepest anguish to God. Each of those expressions is derived from honest relationship with God and is evidence of shared experience, trust, and love. God is always responsive, even when we may feel otherwise. In the mutuality of prayer, answers may not be clear. But salvation is made tangible through the receiving and giving of loving relationship.

Through prayer, we devote ourselves to, participate in, and cooperate with the relational God of love. As we participate and God reciprocates in relationship, love is reincorporated throughout the world. Prayer fans the flame of God's love. Let it burn within each of us!

Relational Theology and the Means of Grace

Dean G. Blevins

Relational theologians believe God designed human beings to be in relationship with God who is, by nature, relational. To be fully human is to be in relationship with the Triune God, participating in God's Trinitarian life. It is to be fully in relationship with other human beings.

While this language sounds inviting (both in our ability to "relate" to God and with others) it begs a question: "How?" Most of us understand what it means to relate to other people. But how do we relate to the God of the universe? How do we relate to One whose majesty is so great that we find it difficult, and sometimes dangerous, to understand in human terms?

Fortunately, God has provided a way to nurture our relationship, one that begins with God's grace but includes our participation. For many Christians, the language of the means of grace describes and defines this approach. When we participate in the means of grace, specific actions, and activities provided by God, we are shaped by those practices. We discern God's relational love for creation and us. And we respond by engaging others and the world redemptively.

What are the Means of Grace?

The language of "the means of grace" finds its roots in the Protestant Reformation and Anglican Church. The General Thanksgiving of the *Book of Common Prayer* (1771) includes the phrase "the means of graceand the hope of glory."[1] John Wesley used the same term to describe a host of specific actions and activities he believed Jesus instituted for the church. These included taking part in the Lord's Supper, praying, fasting, reading scripture, and gathering in community. Wesley also included contextual practices, like reading devotional texts, meeting in small groups, and ministry to the poor.

Each of these practices serve as means of grace, whether more traditional and in line with the church, or more contextual and related to our times. They remind us that God as Father, Son, and Spirit is active, and God mediates God's loving presence and power—grace—through these practices.

John Wesley understood the means of grace to "convey" love much like actions and gifts convey love to a special someone in our lives. Love is eaten in a dinner or transmitted through nerve endings while holding hands. Love emerges and deepens as we discern the intent of these expressions, orient our lives around simple acts of giving and receiving, and seek the well-being of those we love. In the same way, the means of grace are practices that deepen our understanding of God's love. They shape us into the people we desire to be with other people and with God.

In his sermon, "Means of Grace,"[2] Wesley described someone who was not yet a Christian but engaged in hearing scripture, participating in corporate prayer, and conversing with other Christians. Inevitably, this same person encounters Christ in the Lord's Supper, awakening to the fullness of God's love in that action. As persons move through participation in the means of grace, they move through relationships with persons and ultimately with Christ by the guidance of the Holy Spirit.

Practicing the Means of Grace: Living into Relationships

Some simple observations help us understand how we live in and through the means of grace. First, many of the practices are communal in nature. We participate in the means of grace "together" so that God

---

1   *The Book of Common Prayer, And Administration of the Sacraments and Other Rites and Ceremonies of the Church According to the Use of the Church of England.* Oxford: Printed by T. Wright, and IV. Gill, Printers to the University: And sold by S. Crowder, in Paternoster-Row, London; and by IV. Jackson, in Oxford. 1771.

2   Wesley, John. "Means of Grace" in Albert C. Outler, ed. *The Works of John Wesley*, Vol I. Sermons I, 1–33 (Nashville: Abingdon Press, 1738/1984), 376–394.

is relationally involved in the practice, the people, and through God's presence. Second, the means of grace tend to work at several levels of our humanity. They form us to a Christian way of life, revealing to us God's love. They encourage us to reach out to others through redemptive, loving actions.

The means of grace "guide" our participation that deepens our relationship with God and God's people. The means of grace remind us that what we do, as well as who we are, defines our relationships. The practices and habits shape our dispositions, providing a different logic to our daily life.

Finally, we must remember that the means are just that: means, not the end. Each practice should deepen our relationship with God and God's people. If we claim superiority when we practice them or think we have some type of "mastery" over a particular practice, we neglect their end, their purpose. We end up serving ourselves and become distant from God and God's people.

Ultimately, we participate in the means of grace—worship, prayer, hearing scripture, caring for others, the Lord's Supper, etc.—so our lives might also become means of grace for other people and for God's creation. Through these practices, God calls us into loving relationship with God, God's people and God's creation.

The Medium is the Message: Preaching and Relational Theology

T. Scott Daniels

He came and preached peace to you who were far off and peace to those who were near.
—Ephesians 2:17

Preaching (done rightly) is relational by nature. The gospel (understood rightly) is relational by nature. It therefore should not surprise us that when Jesus came to proclaim the initiation of God's reign that he came preaching. I want to argue that preaching is not just one methodology or medium among others that Christ could have used to proclaim the kingdom of God. I believe the relational nature of preaching itself means that it is—and continues to be—the primary medium through which the people of God announce the good news of reconciliation.

In an era increasingly dominated by electronic media, the famous phrase coined by Marshall McLuhan, "The medium is the message," takes on greater significance. The modern world is waking up to the reality that various forms of communication are not "meaning neutral". They carry significant social implications in themselves. For example, a morning newspaper and a nightly television newscast may carry the same stories. But they will, by their nature, tell those stories in different ways. And a culture that receives its information primarily through print media will look different over time than a culture that receives its information only through visual media.

Because it is primarily an image-oriented medium, television is great for sports (think Super Bowl or ESPN). Sporting events contain fast moving images with little sustained dialogue, and they require little intellectual reflection on the part of the viewer. On the other hand, the sustained reasoning necessary for cogent political dialogue makes for lousy television (think CSPAN). Print media—like newspapers or books—is a much better place for sustained, thoughtful, intellectual debate. In fact, political discourse on television is reduced to a series of contrived images and sound bites.

The Apostle Paul and the gospel writers remind us that Christ came preaching. It is certainly possible for a preacher to give a sermon filled with non-relational theology. But when that happens, the message fails to match its medium. I am convinced that the Church has been given a relational medium to proclaim a relational gospel. There are at least three ways in which preaching functions relationally.

First, the message is always incarnated. The Word always becomes flesh. In Galatians 4:4, Paul proclaims that Jesus came "in the fullness of time." I've often thought that if God the Father had been just a little more patient and waited a couple of thousand additional years, he could have sent the Son into a world that could have video-taped his life. Think how much clearer the gospel might have been if we could just download the actual Sermon on the Mount or the trial before Pilate on iTunes. I am obviously being facetious.

I think it is part of God's "fullness of time" purpose that the Church has four different written accounts and interpretations of the events of Christ's life, ministry, death, and resurrection. And we are encouraged and commanded as his people not just to read those accounts. We are told to preach them anew to succeeding generations and in various contexts of the world.

To say it another way, the Word became flesh in the person of Jesus Christ. But it continues to be made flesh in new historical and social settings. The Word became flesh in second-century Gaul through the preaching of Irenaeus. The Word became flesh in fourth- and fifth-century North Africa through the preaching of Augustine. The Word became flesh in eighteenth-century England through the preaching of John Wesley. And I trust the Word becomes flesh again in twenty-first-century Southern California through my preaching.

Secondly, the Word is not just spoken. It is also heard. Proper preaching takes seriously the social location of the one being addressed. One of my favorite missionaries in Church history is the Jesuit Jean de Brebeuf who, in the early seventeenth century, ministered among the

Huron natives located near modern-day Quebec. He is perhaps best known for rewriting the birth narratives of Jesus in not just the language but in social contexts Huron people could understand. In de Brefeuf's translated gospels, Jesus was not born in a stable but in a bark hut. Instead of being wrapped in swaddling clothes, the baby Jesus was wrapped in rabbit fur.

Something in me recognizes this as deeply consistent with a relational understanding of the gospel. The Word that humbled himself to enter into a Bethlehem stable is still willing—through preaching—to enter into a Huron hut, a country chateau, or an inner-city project.

Finally, and most importantly, preaching is relational because, like the Word it proclaims, it invites an uncoerced response. When Paul writes that, "Jesus came preaching peace," I believe he is not just making a statement about the content of the message of Christ. He was making a statement about the very means Jesus chose to embody and extend the peaceable reign of God. To state it more plainly, Jesus chose preaching rather than violence. From his baptism to his death and resurrection, the only sword Jesus bore was "the sword of the Spirit, which is the Word of God" (Eph 6:17).

The Word, as the preached or proclaimed "word," represents the alternative to violence as the means for establishing God's kingdom. The preached Word allows people the freedom of decision, response, and expression. The preached Word requires mutuality and relationship. It necessitates the participation of the one speaking and the one listening. The preached Word does not coerce or control its outcome.

I am convinced that in the kingdom of God the ends do not justify the means. Rather, in the person of Jesus, the distinction between means and ends has been collapsed. Jesus not only proclaims the Way but he is the Way of the kingdom. Therefore, Jesus came preaching not just because it was one methodology among many to use to deliver the message of God's reign. Rather the relational nature of God and his reign requires a medium that is at its core relational.

So I suppose Marshall McLuhan's words about mediums and messages are correct about Jesus too: the medium is message.

Worship as Relational Renewal and Redemption of the World

Brent D. Peterson

W hy do we worship? What purpose does it serve? How does it participate in the Kingdom of God? This chapter suggests that:

1. Communal worship is the primary means by which persons become more human.
2. Communal worship celebrates and participates in God's redemption of the world.

Before exploring these two primary postures, I want to explore some conversation on the image of God and what worship is not.

Image of God: Created in Love for Love

The story of Genesis proclaims that God created humans in God's image, out of love for love. Created in God's image is an invitation to love God, love oneself, love other humans, and care for creation as an extension of the first three. Jesus declares that the primary purpose of the law is to help persons love in this way, to be more fully human. A scribe asked Jesus what he regarded as the greatest commandment. Jesus responded with the *Shema* from Deuteronomy 6:4–5, "You shall love the Lord your God with all your heart, and with all of your soul." In addition, Christ offered the second most important commandment to confirm the full vision of the image of God, "You shall love your neighbor as yourself" (Mt 22:36–40).

As the human drama unfolds in the early chapters of Genesis, humans unfortunately elevate their own desires. They not only disobey

76

God, they kill other humans out of jealousy. Sinning is a failure to love and a disfiguring of God's image. To sin is a failure to be human. Sin is a relational rupture, a disease within humanity that must be healed.

God provided Israel a means to be reconciled: the embodied worship of the sacrificial system.[1] Sadly, for some, the practices of this embodied worship became the focus. They were not accompanied with hearts of repentance. Those who rejected God's reconciliation were rejecting God's invitation to healing and renewal. Outward forms of worship cannot substitute for inward penitence.

Wal-Mart Worship

Isaiah announced that because of the hardness of Israel's heart, God found Israel's worship detestable. "I have had enough of your burnt offerings of rams and the fat of fed beasts; I do not delight in the blood of bulls, or of lambs, or of goats" (1:11). God continues this rejection by noting that their acts of worship (their liturgy) have made God weary. When they stretch out hands in worship, "I will hide my eyes from you; even though you make many prayers, I will not listen; your hands are full of blood" (1:15).

The Israelites' worship was not authentic. They offered bulls, goats, and incense to pay for their sins, while their hearts were unrepentant. The Israelites treated worship like a Wal-Mart transaction of forgiveness. We do the same when we sin, go to church to pay off our debt, and yet have little desire to change our behaviors or sinful ways.

God's aversion to the sacrifice of animals with unrepentant hearts is found throughout the Psalter, the Minor Prophets, and in the gospels. God desires that persons offer themselves to God. This is to be their primary liturgy-work in worship (See Rom 12:1–2, Hos 6:6, Ps 51:16–17). Worship that God desires is not empty or meaningless ritual. God finds it abominable when corpses go through the motions of praising and praying with heart and mind closed to love.

Worship to Become More Fully Human

How can persons become human again (love God, self, and others)? How can they be healed from the disease of sin?

---

1   Leviticus 1:4–9 describes how the burnt offering makes atonement and 4:3–13 describes the atonement needed for unintentional sins that had been committed.

I believe communal worship is a primary way for this relational healing to occur. In communal worship, God gathers persons to remind them why they were created. God reminds them they are still loved, that they must confess their sins, repent, and seek forgiveness from God and one another. In this, God's healing presence works in their lives.

Christians must remember from Isaiah that God is most interested in persons offering their broken hearts and spirits to God. God is not much interested in our simply offering outward actions for others to see. As Christians offer themselves to God in humility and brokenness, God offers transforming forgiveness. This offer enables persons to love God, themselves, and others more deeply.

The Israelites embodied this communal emphasis of worship through the celebration of eating meals together. The Offering of Well-Being celebrated and renewed the covenants made between the worshipers and with the Lord. This emphasis of the meal in communal worship was borne among the Israelites, central for Jesus' ministry, and continues in the church.[2]

Worship as Participation in the Renewal of Creation

Communal worship contains a vision beyond personal healing. As persons find healing, they are sent from communal worship each Lord's Day to embody relationally the grace, hope, and forgiveness of God in all corners of the world.

Immediately following God's condemnation of the Israelites worship in Isaiah 1:15, God announces the full hope of the preparation needed for communal worship and picture of a life full of worship to God. "Wash yourselves; make yourselves clean; remove the evil of your doings from before my eyes; cease to do evil, learn to do good; seek justice, rescue the oppressed, defend the orphan, plead for the widow" (1:16–17).

Communal worship not only enables humans to find healing from the disease of sin. In it, God enables, empowers, and sends Christians out by the Spirit to care for fellow humans who are hurting and broken. This is not a general call to anyone. Just as Jesus spent most of his time with

---

2   Jesus' meals are scattered all over the New Testament. Jesus' table fellowship with the disciples and with "tax collectors and sinners" provided a model for the church. The young church carried on this fellowship as both a renewal with God and one another and a means of evangelism. See Acts 2:46–47.

the oppressed, downcast, and marginalized, so too should the Church go with the Spirit.

Going with the Spirit to collaborate with God's work to rescue the oppressed and defend the orphan becomes an extension of communal worship. Just as distasteful as Wal-Mart forgiveness is, so too is thinking we earn healing by "caring for the poor." The church cares for the downtrodden as an act of doxology: thankful worship. This continues and extends the Church's liturgy during the week. This worship of love and hope throughout the week is empowered by the Spirit in communal worship. And those who worship believe they participate in the kingdom of God coming more fully to earth.

Communal worship not only participates in the further redemption of creation. It celebrates in hope that the Kingdom of God will come in fullness. This confidence offers the church hope and joy that it may love God, others, and itself so fiercely that it will love even to laying down one's life for another.

Communal worship celebrates and participates in God's redemption of the world. Humans are created in God's image *for* love: to love God, oneself, others, and to care for creation. Communal worship enables persons to become more fully healed, to be human, in relationship. Such love participates in God's relational restoration of creation.

Spiritual Formation & Relational Theology

Douglas S. Hardy

Spiritual formation is the process by which Christians become more like Jesus. The New Testament often calls it *sanctification*, because it is empowered and guided by the Holy Spirit. We can describe this process using other equally helpful phrases, such as "spiritual development" or "maturing in Christ" or "growing in holiness." I like the term "spiritual formation" because these words are deeply rooted in Scripture. Each expresses something important about how the authors of the Bible understood the relationship between God and human beings. Let's begin with the word "spiritual."

What is "Spiritual"?

In the opening chapter of the book of Genesis, we read, "the Spirit of God swept over the face of the waters" (Gen 1:2). [1] When "God said, 'Let us make humankind in our image, according to our likeness'" (1:26), God who is Spirit made people to be spiritual. They were created to be like God through relationship with the Creator.

In Genesis chapter 3, we learn that this special relationship was altered by human disobedience. God first responded to disobedience by calling to Adam and Eve, "Where are you?'" (3:9). In the chapters that follow, we find God providing for people and their children. Despite their sin, God meets them, helps them, and seeks their help (Gen 4, 6–9).

---

1   All Scripture quotations are taken from the *New Revised Standard Version*, Division of Christian Education of the National Council of the Churches of Christ in the United States of America (New York: Oxford University Press, 1989).

God not only created us for relationship, God also seeks to restore and strengthen that relationship when strained.

The relational God who continually seeks us out became known most fully in Jesus Christ. It was Christ who "came to seek out and to save the lost" (Lk 19:10). God is also fully known in the Holy Spirit, who "helps us in our weakness . . . [and] intercedes for the saints" (Rom 8:26–27).

We are spiritual first because we have been breathed into being by God. This is true of all people. We are spiritual in a second and explicitly Christian sense when we respond faithfully to God. This process strengthens the relationship. We might picture it this way:

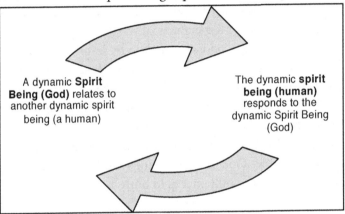

A dynamic **Spirit Being (God)** relates to another dynamic spirit being (a human)

The dynamic **spirit being (human)** responds to the dynamic Spirit Being (God)

What is "Formation"?

Now let's consider the second word, "formation." This biblical word is also found at the beginning of Genesis where we read, "The LORD God formed man from the dust of the ground" (Gen 2:7). The Psalmist exclaimed that God "formed my inward parts ...[and] knit me together in my mother's womb" (Ps 139:13). The prophet Isaiah says God affirms we are "the people whom I formed for myself" (Isa 43:21).

Not surprising, the apostle Paul uses formation language when talking about Christian believers: "My little children, for whom I am again in the pain of childbirth until Christ is formed in you" (Gal 4:19). Formation is best described by gestation and birthing images. What could be more relational than that? Bodies give "form" or "shape" to the spiritual beings that we are, allowing us to be in relationship to each other and God. We live a spiritual life through our bodies, our minds, our emotions, our desires, and our will.

Christian Spiritual Formation

Putting the two words together—*spiritual* and *formation*—helps us to see the promise and the challenge of being in relationship to a relational God. Christian spiritual formation is the process, enabled by the Holy Spirit of God, of renewing and strengthening our God-like *spiritual* identity by being *formed* into Christlikeness. The process is spiritual, because it deals with our created personhood in relation to God. It is formational, because it takes a specific shape in our personal bodies and the community of bodies with whom we live in this world, moving us in a specific direction toward a specific goal.

What is the goal? It is best summed up by Jesus' instruction to "love the Lord your God with all your heart, and with all your soul, and with all your strength, and with all your mind; and your neighbor as yourself" (Lk 10:27). Of course, this is exactly what Jesus himself did. Our love for God and for others becomes part of God's love for the world. And in our loving, Christ is more fully formed in us. In other words, our responsiveness enables God to be more fully God in and through us. Like any real relationship, the influence is in both directions.

Relational Practices for Spiritual Formation

Easier said than done. Doing is an essential aspect of being spiritually formed. The first and foundational doing is God's. What God has done for us in Jesus Christ and continues to do for us through the Holy Spirit makes spiritual formation possible.

Because Christian spiritual formation is an expression of relationship, we must partner with God in the doing. Paul says it well: "... [W]ork out your own salvation with fear and trembling; for it is God who is at work in you, enabling you both to will and to work for his good pleasure" (Phil 2:12–13).

How do we "work out" spiritually? By engaging in practices that, over time, put us in a place to be "taught by God to love one another" (1 Thes 4:19). As we open ourselves to God's love, we learn to love others. As we love others, our capacity to love God deepens. Consider, therefore, the following practices of love. They are also referred to as "spiritual disciplines" or "means of grace."

Praying is the language of relationship between God and those who faithfully respond. Jesus' first words of the Lord's Prayer were the very intimate "Our Father [Abba] ..." (Mt 6:9). God not only wants our prayers, God sometimes needs our prayers to help fulfill God's will on earth.

Reading, listening to, and *meditating on Scripture* are also essential practices for Christian spiritual formation. We engage Scripture to be addressed by God. The Bible is God's message to us, inviting our response in return.

Fasting from the good things in our lives—food, sex, entertainment, work—guards our relationship with God from being displaced by other gods. Setting and keeping these boundaries also frees us to love others in a healthy way.

Serving others expresses our love for God and strengthens community bonds.

As Jesus demonstrated on the cross, the greatest service is to "love your enemies" (Mt 5:44). This may be the most powerful way to affirm the value of our God-given potential for relationship.

Pastoral Ministry

Jeren Rowell

Several years ago, I set out to study pastors who were enjoying long tenure with their congregations. I was looking for the strategy or the skill set that enabled these pastors to thrive in their assignments. Finding little correlation between ability and long tenure, I realized that one repeated theme did find its way through the responses of nearly all pastors interviewed. In one way or another they said, "When it comes down to it, I love my people and I know they love me."

Healthy pastoral ministry can only rightly find its moorings in a theology of love. All other possibilities finally collapse under the weight of spiritual leadership that is the life and work of a pastor. The pastoral office, understood from relational theology, is not about position or power. It's about self-sacrificing love that prefers and seeks God's best for the other. Congregational life ordered from this foundation becomes an authentic expression of the kingdom of God in the world.

Practically, then, we may begin to think about how this works out in the daily ministry of pastors. For example, pastoral ministry that finds its foundation in love directly challenges many popular notions of what pastors are to be and do. For some time, the language and literature on pastoral ministry borrowed from business themes to frame the work of pastor in terms of the corporate chief executive officer. Some pastors began to use organizational management language and structures to order neatly the messy work of shepherding. We tried to shore up a sagging sense of popular esteem by talking and acting like the local bank president or corporate executive, only to find ourselves distanced from many people and places where Jesus-style ministry takes place. Gladly, a recovery is underway as pastors shift from cultural leadership models to the person and work of Jesus of Nazareth.

As the Gospels rehearse the story of Jesus, some key themes emerge that give meaningful definition to what it means to be a pastor. Among these themes I have especially noticed the following: *humility* (birth in a stable and life as a peasant), *solidarity* (identification with the poor and abused), *compassion* (acts of mercy and healing), *integrity* (no compromise with worldly systems of power), and *sacrifice* (laying down of one's life in service to others). Certainly, we could name other significant themes. These are essential in terms of how the life and teaching of Jesus becomes foundational for healthy pastoral theology.

Humility calls us to challenge the accepted cultural notion that success is about winning (with the implication that some necessarily lose). It reminds us to view every good thing as gift rather than as just reward. We work not only to provide or gain but also to contribute and bless. These ideas shape the pastor's work. They are ways work is understood in the congregation, both gathered in worship and sent into the world.

Solidarity is closely related and teaches us that daily decisions are never chosen in safe isolation. What we do influences others in ways we usually will not see.

Compassion shapes our service as it moves us from acts of duty to acts of love. It is one thing to work for the healing of the lost and broken from an ethical obligation to do so. But the deepest acts of healing seem to rise from a grace-enabled sense of identity with those who suffer.

Integrity calls us to account for authentic agreement between our words and our deeds. It is not the idea of living from our convictions flawlessly. It is that we are willing to confess our shortcomings so we might repent and learn. Integrity demands of a Christ-follower that the worldly systems of power and influence give way to the Jesus-style power of laying down one's life.

This is *sacrifice*, which is a decision long before it is an opportunity. A sacrificial mindset enables one to respond intuitively in a moment in ways that demonstrate a life lived in service to others rather than in protection of one's own interests.

These values may seem to some lofty and idealistic. Rising from a relationship of pastor and people that is characterized by covenantal love, however, these values are real and practical. They come into play in the momentous decisions of congregational life. They come into play (perhaps especially) in the seemingly inconsequential decisions that are part of life together.

Another way to think about pastoral work that emerges from biblical images is to remember the classically defined offices of Christ, namely: prophet, priest, and shepherd-king. *Prophet* speaks in part of the role of truth telling in the midst of a people. Jesus is described in John's gospel as one who was "full of grace and truth" (Jn 1:14). By grace, the presence and work of a pastor can become a healing balm in the lives of broken people. This work includes the commitment to speak truth in loving ways that expose that which is compromised and false not only in the world, but in the lives of God's people.

Priest is the most loved form of our ministry. We gather God's people in the name of our risen Lord Jesus Christ under the power of the Holy Spirit. We exhort people who have lost their true identity to worship God and thus become "righted" again. We proclaim the Word of the Lord and joyfully announce the Gospel. We lead our people in prayers of confession, repentance, and covenant. We help our people use the divine grace through the gifts of sacrament, and we pronounce the blessing of God upon them in Jesus' name. What beautiful work indeed!

The image of *shepherd-king* speaks to the most common aspects of our work. Although we are most comfortable with the shepherd metaphor, the idea of king should not be lost. This is not a "lording over" role. It is the work of loving administration, whereby our leadership helps create structures of ministry that promote the common good. We are spiritual leaders, theologians in residence, administrative heads of the organization, and mouthpieces of God. These roles are not things we embrace from our own abilities. These are gifts God gives to build up the church; they are charges placed on us by the weight of our ordination vows. The ways in which we exercise these authorities will lead either to communities of peace and security, or to communities of chaos and abuse.

These acts of pastoral ministry form the work. But they become much more than mere technology when done in a way that reflects the love of the Good Shepherd who said, "The good shepherd lays down his life for the sheep" (Jn 10:11). So pastors pray, study the Scriptures, and live life with the people in ways that become a living sign of a God who loves "with an everlasting love" (Jer 31:3).

IV.
Ethics and Justice in Relational Perspective

Ethics as Relational

Kevin Twain Lowery

I often ask my students whether action or motive is more important to ethics. They typically conclude that although action may be the overriding concern when the stakes are high enough, we generally regard motive as central to ethics. For instance, although the doctor's competence is what we value most when faced with a life-threatening illness or operation, we believe that the doctors with the highest ethical standards are those who genuinely care about being competent. Physicians' personal ethical standards reflect their motives.

I press my students further, asking them why we consider motives to be such an important part of ethics. Some reply, "It's more difficult to change motive than action. That's why we value it more." Indeed, whereas actions quite often can be changed quickly (even through pressure), motives are typically shaped over time. Other students answer, "A person with a good motive is more likely to do the right thing consistently." Yes, motive is the foundation of action, and this gives it a certain priority over action.

Nevertheless, we still have not reached the heart of the matter. I continue, "So, if I buy my wife roses every Valentine's Day, do you think that my consistency is what makes my motives moral?" At this point, it all starts to click for them. "No, what makes it moral is love!"

There it is. Love is at the heart of ethics. In I Corinthians 13, Paul tells us that the value of ethical action is shallow and superficial without the motive of love. People can "do the right thing" out of self-interest alone. However, this kind of action is only ethical in the sense of being beneficial to others. Besides, selfish people only "do the right thing" for what they get out of it. The "right thing" is merely a means to the end of pleasing oneself. In contrast, the end (i.e., goal) of love is the well-being and happiness of the other.

Thomas Aquinas defined love as the desire to be in union with the other, and this expresses an important truth about love. Love aims at relationship. We want to be in relationship with those we love, and we want to be loved by them in return. The goal of ethics is thus to develop and promote relationship, namely, our relationship with God and our relationship with others. This is why Christ indicates that the love commandments (i.e., loving God wholeheartedly and loving one's neighbor as oneself) encapsulate the rest of God's commandments. It is also why the pursuit of holiness is interconnected with the pursuit of peace with all people, both far and near (Heb 12:14). As John Wesley said, there is no holiness but social holiness.

Not only is ethics ultimately about our relationship with God, it is unhealthy to view them as conflicted. Essentially, ethics and spirituality are two aspects of the same thing. Remember Jesus's words, "Whatever you have done unto the least of these brothers of mine, you have done it unto me." (Mt 25:40) Yes, our service to God is more than just being nice to others, but serving God never entails disobeying the command that Christ has given us to love one another. God does not command us to love and then contradict himself by commanding us to act in ways that are unloving.

Some people make the mistake of separating ethics into two categories: natural (day-to-day) ethics and religious ("true") ethics. Others claim that something is right simply because God has commanded it. It should be obvious how this line of thinking can lead to some pretty dangerous conclusions. History is strewn with atrocities that have been committed in God's name. Many problems arise when people fail to recognize the relational nature of ethics. It is even worse when they use God's name to justify immoral acts, because they become too self-assured and refuse to listen to reason.

No matter how we describe and systematize ethics (rules, goals, virtues, natural law, etc.), it always aims at relationship. Ethics is not a set of abstract standards we must uphold. Rather, God's commands are for our good and for the good of others. In fact, they are for the good of all creation. Theologically speaking, ethics is relational, because God is relational.

Ethics recognizes the connection between our relationship with God and our relationship with one another. Scripture addresses this numerous times, especially the gospels and I John. Love for God and love for neighbor go hand in hand. Granted, God has preeminence over all. However, when we recognize the universality of God's love, it becomes evident why love for God always includes love for others.

In a nutshell, ethics seeks to promote the well-being and happiness of others. And this is what God wants us to do. This sounds rather simple, but understanding how to accomplish this can be difficult.

Human beings are complex creatures, so our "well-being" and "happiness" can likewise be quite complex and intricate. It's hard to know what is in one's own best interest, let alone know the best interest of others.

In addition, we live with the expectations of others. Many people have trouble distinguishing ethical matters from societal norms. Many things considered wrong are simply social taboos. The only supposed "harm" they cause is the offense that they bring. The reason that people are offended is that the group tells them that they are supposed to be offended.

We must work to discern what truly affects well-being and happiness, because these are the truly ethical matters. Nevertheless, the relational aspect of ethics does not allow us casually to disregard the feelings of others, even when those feelings are not grounded in sound judgment. This is exactly what Paul has in mind when he discusses private conscience in Romans 14.

Of course, each person is unique. This means that each person's well-being and happiness are likewise unique in some way. Similarly, relationships differ. We do not relate to everyone in the same way, neither do we have the same level of intimacy in all of our relationships. Our responsibilities to others vary, and we have greater responsibility to some than to others.

In general, each relationship entails a degree of love and a level of responsibility. These degrees and levels correspond with the nature of each relationship. As world citizens, for example, we have responsibilities to the people and creatures that share this world with us. That includes responsibility to the environment and the resources on which we all depend. All of earths' citizens share these responsibilities. We also have personal relationships that are more intimate and carry a greater weight of responsibility. For instance, I have a unique relationship with my wife and children. I am the only person who can fulfill the responsibilities associated with those relationships.

In some ways, humans are all the same. Relationships also share common characteristics. To the extent that humans and circumstances are the same, ethics is the same. On the other hand, people and relationships are unique, as we just noted. This implies that ethics is also flexible and contextual.

Consider the following example. What does it mean to be a good parent (in an ethical sense)? Some aspects of parenting are generally relevant for all parents. For instance, children have the same basic physiological and psychological needs, and ethical parenting requires these needs to be met. Nevertheless, each child is different, so parenting is not a "one size fits all" affair.

The key thing to remember is that ethics is relational, so our task is to promote relationships. This requires us to promote the well-being and happiness of those with whom we have some relationship. In the final analysis, that includes everyone. In a very real and deep sense, we are all related to one another.

The Cross or Caesar? A Postcolonial Query

Gabriel Salguero

A Woman and a Horse Called Imperialism

In April 2004, one of the featured stories on *The Today Show* focused on the youngest female trainer in the Kentucky Derby. Kristin Mulhall, a 21-year-old woman, was saddling a partially blind horse called Imperialism. When I saw this story I thought, "What a fitting image for how many Christians do theology and live out being church."

Many views of God, church, being human, and how the church ought to be in the world are, regrettably, informed by a sightless ambition. *The Today Show's* reminder of a myopic imperialism is a fitting place to begin a dialogue with people interested in relational theology and postcolonial concerns. The Church should never ride a partially blind horse called Imperialism. Rather, the Church is called to be a loving community of saints that reflect God's love and justice in the world.

What do we mean by imperialism? Imperialism represents the networks of power that homogenize or co-opt voices in order to maintain their control over them. Empire is "a new global and universal order that seeks to encompass all of life."[1] Empire crucified Christ, Peter, and martyred the early saints. Empire is deeply impersonal, because it does not seek the good of others but only its own selfish ends.

Imperial ambitions are anti-God in that they seek to use people for the growth of empire, be that land, riches, people, buildings, or other so-called treasures. An imperialistic faith is not interested in people except as consumers, objects, or producers. God, on the other hand, is in a relentless loving pursuit of humanity out of selfless love.

---

1   Michael Hardt & Antonio Negri, *Empire* (Cambridge, Mass.: Harvard University Press, 2000), 46.

Indigenous people offer classic critiques of imperial Christianity, sometimes called Constantinian Christianity. When the Christians came to these people, they had the land and Christians had the Bible. When Christians left, they had the land and indigenous people had only the Bible. Such transactional Christianity undermines human interdependence and loving relationships. This imperialist blind horse cannot carry a faith that follows the Crucified Jesus.

"What's Love Got to do with It?" A Postcolonial Call

Those unfamiliar with postcolonial theology sometimes wonder if such theological reflection and action are necessary. They ask, "What does this have to do with God and what it means to follow Jesus Christ?"

Postcolonial theology is an invitation to focus on how a relational God models for us how *to be and act* in the world. Just as theology and Scripture readings that focus on power may be complicit with colonizing enterprises, postcolonial theology can provide more loving theologies of the church and mission. At its best, Christian theology promotes human dignity and systemic justice in the here and now. Theologies that seriously consider the view of the underside of history provide a broader analysis of the harmful impact idolatrous nationalism and imperial ambitions have on our understandings of God and how we act in the world. Prophetic voices like Dietrich Bonhoeffer, Martin Luther King, Jr., and Bartolomé de Las Casas warn against theological reflection that treats the other as object or less than human.

Postcolonial scriptural reading reminds us that theology cannot be divorced from the real lives and deaths of indigenous peoples, slaves, women, children, and the poorest of the poor in the world. God is love. Love attempts to care for all people. Love considers how power affects the lives of people.

Postcolonial theology takes seriously the impact and influence of imperialism, colonialism, and neo-colonialism on all of life. It points to political, cultural, aesthetic, and geographical boundaries that work against God's loving and just actions in the world. It considers people first as citizens of the Kingdom of God. In short, postcolonial theology provides a loving alternative to imperial Christianity, namely a love-oriented, servant-minded Christianity.

Anti-imperial Christian faith calls us prophetically and lovingly to act more like Christ-crucified than Caesar-enthroned. Postcolonial theologians seek to unmask a faith that sees others and creation as objects, producers, or targets. Imperial faith denies a Gospel that at its heart is about loving people and acknowledging one's worth as the image of God.

Throughout history, many Christians have followed the way of empire and not the way of the Cross. Some of us have coveted power, used people, loved Mammon, and despised service. Postcolonial theology highlights that stream of the Christian witness that has loved the neighbor over power, given more than it received, and followed the downward mobility of the Crucified Christ over the ambitions of the Caesars, Pharaohs, and Führers.

The God we Christians profess is personal and is profoundly concerned with our plight. We are not objects, targets, or products to God. We are the image of God called into loving relationship. Relationality is rooted in a God who from the beginning has been relational, and the Cross of Christ concretely manifests the type of love-relation God desires.

The Cross: A Critique of Imperial Power

We must recover the scandal of the cross. If there is anything the Cross of Christ reminds us it is that Christ is not Caesar. The Cross of Jesus has too often been co-opted, domesticated, and commoditized. It continues to face the threat of co-optation.

Yet, the message of the Cross still speaks. St. Paul speaks of unearthing its message: "For the message of the cross is foolishness ... but we proclaim Christ crucified, a stumbling block to Jews and foolishness to Gentiles" (1 Cor 1:18a, 23). From the earliest of Christian writings to this day, the Cross continues to be a scandal and foolishness both to the nations and the religious insiders. St. Paul underlines the danger Christians face, for they may be tempted to follow the example of "rulers of this age ... who crucified the Lord of glory" (1 Cor 2:8).

Our critique of power and wisdom can only be understood if we recover the scandal and foolishness of the Cross. The Cross is absolute power in absolute service to the other. Jesus' act of surrender is a call to the Church to resist what Friedrich Nietzsche called "the will to power." Christ's reign emerges whenever those who seek greatness become a servant with a basin and a towel.

The way of the Cross is the anti-dote to Caesar-hungry faith. It sees others as brothers and sisters, not as slaves and strangers. In ancient days, the power-hungry often sided with the Roman Empire to secure their fortunes, while the masses yearned for legitimate authority that loved them unconditionally. The crucifixion of Jesus Christ is a postcolonial critique of religious complicity with empire's ideas and violence.

Conclusion

The "post" in postcolonial is a call, a vision, a prophecy. "Post" means that we hope. We can dream about and work for a day in which God's shalom reign of Isaiah 11 is a reality. We can anticipate the lion and the lamb dwelling together.

"Post" means that love conquers our appetites to colonize, enslave, and control. "Post" in postcolonial means that God's love will bring to its knees all the kingdoms of this earth and establish a reign of love and justice for all of creation.

We, the followers of a Christ who was executed by an empire, are called to live and work for the postcolonial loving reign of God.

Social Justice and Relational Theology

Brian K. Postlewait

Social justice always begs the questions: whose justice, which society? History books chronicle the quest for justice among peoples. Social justice is an ever-moving target. It grows and evolves at varying speeds. From abolition of slavery to workers' rights, from child labor to gender equality, we have and continue to stretch our social structures to fit our vision for social justice.

The scriptures, together with the history of the church, mirror this changing and evolving pattern for social justice. God cares deeply about how communities structure their common life. The scriptures give witness to the call and quest for social justice among God's chosen people. They beckon us to do justice and love mercy. God's people take up the call for justice and challenge societies to embrace God's vision.

Relational theology allows us to account for this evolving vision of justice. God's relationship to human beings is sufficient and unfolding. God joins us where we are situated within our social and cultural reality. And God works with humanity to fulfill God's purposes while preserving human agency.

As we journey with God, our vision of justice gains expansive potential. In fact, through the lens of relational theology, we are confronted by the idea that God and the witness of the scriptures call us to even greater mercy, compassion, and justice.

The term *social justice* itself generates deep feelings. Some experience passion for a cause. Some recall memories of dramatic movements of history that change perceptions and reorganize power structures. But others wince in discomfort, skeptical of hidden political agendas.

All these feelings arise out of deep concern for how we human beings structure our lives together.

These reactions to the phrase "social justice" make messy the work of pulling the phrase into the biblical story and the task of Christian theology. But a few things are clear. First, the biblical narrative defines a God-centered agenda for social justice. Second, the people of God take God's vision and implement it. And, third, as a result God's vision for social justice, "shalom" unfolds.

The biblical narrative defines a God-centered agenda for social justice. Beginning in Genesis, God hears the cries of the Hebrews and has compassion on them. They are enslaved, and God responds to their call for help. As the Hebrew people become Israelites, God encourages them to remember their hardships as a motivation to care for others: Fight the cause of the oppressed. Care for the widow and orphan. Feed the hungry. Welcome the stranger and alien.

As Israel gains wealth, power, and strength, voices from within the community begin to criticize their lack of concern for those on the margins. When national calamity strikes (war, famine, exile), a call for justice often becomes the diagnosis of where the people went wrong. Likewise, this call often becomes a way to correct the problems. The prophet Micah, for instance, commands the people to "do justice, to love mercy, and to walk humbly."

When exiled in Babylon, God's call for justice clearly extends beyond the Israelites' own internal needs to the entire capital city. We hear echoes of God's promise to Abraham, "I will make you a great nation ... I will bless you...to be a blessing to others." Jeremiah calls the once-enslaved, then free, now exiled people to pursue justice among a strange people in a strange land. "Build houses ... plant gardens ... increase ... and seek the *shalom* of the city ... pray for it ... by seeking *shalom* you will find your own *shalom*" (author's translation with emphases added).

This vision of "shalom" is a recurring call for a God-centered agenda of justice. We get glimpses of the purpose of this vision in both Old and New Testaments—a society of garden cities and sustainable lives, where lions, lambs, children, and snakes are at peace.

The people of God take God's vision and implement it. Jesus gives new license to an expanding vision of justice. He begins by expanding the benefits of the kingdom of God toward "outsiders." Now, even the religiously inferior, the ill, the blind, the deaf, the crippled, and others on the margins of society are included in God's agenda for justice. The people of God take this vision and run with it. Jewish Christian communities lean toward inclusion of Gentiles, even Roman soldiers. Paul begins to flirt with abolition of slavery and gender equality.

The early church seems to embrace a spirituality of social justice. Taking the vision of Matthew 25 seriously, they welcome the stranger, feed the hungry, cloth the naked, visit the imprisoned. They believe when doing so they meet Jesus in distressed disguise. Roman Christians attend to dead bodies left to rot in the street, believing they were caring for the broken body of Jesus himself.

Early Christian communities took this God-centered agenda of justice and propelled it into society. They worked for the care of widows and orphans, contended for the dignified treatment of the dead, and pioneered community-based healthcare. Propelled by the worship of God in community through their understanding of the scriptures and the teachings of Jesus, they applied a God-centered agenda for justice into a call for social justice of all.

Centuries later John Wesley preached heart renewal and worked for the abolition of slavery. He called for prison reform and worked to create a health system for the poor. Christian leaders like Wesley planted a God-centered agenda for justice into new fertile soil.

As a result, God's vision for social justice, "shalom," continues to unfold. It influences new movements for justice in our own time. In recent past, Christians worked for the abolition of slavery, child protection, women's suffrage, prohibition, civil rights for African Americans, protection for the unborn, nuclear disarmament, and most recently, creation care.

The Christian vision of justice has always outpaced a strict reading of the scriptures. When the church takes the whole witness of the scriptures into account, it embraces an expanding vision for social justice. The scriptures and church tradition inspire this vision for justice. But we must take God's vision and do something with it. So, with humility, we seek God's leading by the power of the Spirit. In the end, we walk with humility, knowing God's call for love, mercy, compassion, and justice may ultimately be deeper and wider than we first imagine.

Relational theology opens our thinking to envision a quest for social justice that grows and evolves within the context of our relationship with God and others. Let us seek justice, love and mercy, and walk humbly with our God.

Relational Dimensions of Feminist Theology
Diane Leclerc

eminist theology affirms the basic tenets of relational theology: God is deeply and reciprocally connected to humanity. It especially affirms that God is as deeply connected to women as men, and it calls women to become all God created them to be. Feminist theology affirms that to be Christian affects our relationships with humanity and other parts of creation.[1] It especially affirms that God's intention is mutual love between human beings, who themselves seek the full dignity of *all* persons. God's empathetic and kenotic (self-emptying) love makes this possible.

To talk more specifically about feminist theology's connection to relational theology, it might be good to get clarity on feminism. Many people do not realize that feminism does not have a single definition or uniform expression. How one defines feminism depends on other positions that a person holds.

For example, "secular feminism" is connected to "secularism" and its many propositions. Some think this is the only form of feminism. But there are Christian expressions as well. The basic premise of all feminism is the full equality of all people, regardless of gender. This is obviously a statement about relationships. What "Christianizes" feminism is the belief that equality is what God intends and what God enables through love.

---

1   As feminist theology advanced, something called "Eco-Feminism" developed. This is the belief that just as we are to seek the dignity of women, we are also to seek respect and dignity for creation.

Christian forms of feminism (although certainly varied and nuanced) generally include at least five ideas. All have relational implications.

First, Christian feminism affirms that God created man and woman as equals, both created in the image of God.

Second, only after the fall were women subjected to men. This subjection was not God's will, but a result of sin.

Third, God desires to reverse the effects of the fall in this present life.

Fourth, at least for some feminists, Pentecost has an *egalitarian* effect. In other words, in Pentecost all persons are called to all the offices and practices of the church. And this inclusive nature of the Spirit should continue to this day.

Fifth, Paul should be read as an early church "feminist." Whereas some Christian traditions interpret Paul as reinforcing the subordination of women, many Christian feminists see Paul as opening doors to women to serve in his churches. He expected women to pray and to prophecy. And Paul said, "there is no Jew nor Greek, slave nor free, male and female, for you are all one in Christ Jesus" (Gal 3:28).

Paul says that there is no difference in value for persons who are in Christ. But is he implying no difference *at all*? One of the main questions of "feminist theory," which inform "feminist theology," is the question of whether men and women are essentially the same or different. This is another place where feminist theology meets *relational* theology. Some believe women are more "naturally" relational than men. Is this true? One implication of this, if it is true, is that women have a unique and important voice in theology.

One early feminist wanted to say exactly that. In what becomes a very important article (first published in 1960), Valerie Saiving suggests that theology has neglected women's experiences and perspectives. She implies that theology done only from a male perspective is necessarily incomplete, and traditionally Christian theology has been "done" only by men.

Saiving recognizes that "it would be ridiculous to deny that there is a structure of experience common to both men and women, so that we may legitimately speak of the 'human situation' without reference to sexual identity." But goes on to say that "the only question is whether we have described the human situation correctly by taking account of the experiences of both sexes."[2] Feminists since Saiving have assumed that women have something to contribute to the theological task as *women*.

Despite the fact that feminism has more recently been challenged by "post-structuralism,"[3] many feminist theologians affirm women's relational intuitions. We can also point out that many feminist theologians hold to the premises of *relational theology*.

One feminist theologian is especially noteworthy. Mildred Bangs Wynkoop was a theologian whose colleagues in the theology faculties in which she taught were entirely men. Her context was the Holiness tradition in the middle to late 20th century. Her theology sounded very different from most of her male counterparts. In historical retrospect, we now affirm that what she was offering to the dialogue about holiness was its *relational* components. She should certainly be counted as a relational theologian.

In an early attempt to articulate her emerging relational theology of holiness, Wynkoop penned an unpublished work titled, "An Existential Interpretation of the Doctrine of Holiness."[4] What she finds attractive in existentialism is a radical honesty about human life. She combined this with her reflection on Wesley's early Methodism and its extreme practicality. This combination led her to conclude that the Christian life, and specifically holiness, must breathe. Its heart must beat. Its feet must walk in the footsteps of Christ, who walked not only with God, but in community.

Wynkoop believed holiness only exists in its expression, which is love. By taking existentialism's "humanism" and putting it in dialogue with the power of God's grace to make us loving persons and communities, "existentialism" becomes "relationalism" in Wynkoop. We express love in relationships, namely our relationship with God and others. The purpose for which we are created is not to "glorify God and enjoy him forever," thought Wynkoop. It is to *love* God with our entire being and to *love* our

---

2   Valerie Saiving, "The Human Situation: A Feminine View," *Journal of Religion* 40 (1960): 100–112.

3   As feminist theory met post-structuralism, a very ironic outcome occurred. Some previous feminist theorists and the theologians now identify themselves as "post-feminists." Post-structuralism "deconstructed" gender itself. There is no longer a singular category of "woman." Ironically, this theoretical conclusion brought the much-needed work of the feminist movement to an abrupt halt.

4   This was written in 1958; some the material from this work makes it into her most important book, *A Theology of Love*, published in 1972.

neighbors as ourselves. In fact, she believed this human potential for love *is* the *imago dei*.

Feminist theologians like Wynkoop, me, and others believe holiness as relational love lives only in the "dynamic" between God and humans. And holiness is possible among human relationships because of God. This means sin is also best understood in relational terms: sin is anti-love. Holiness is found most clearly when we love, as God first loves us, in the context of genuine divine and human relationships. Love always works for the full dignity of the other, whether "Jew or Greek, slave or free, male and female."

Feminist and relational theologies at their best affirm that God *is* love. And we are also to love each other.

Jewish-Christian Dialogue

Marty Alan Michelson

C hristian theology celebrates that Jesus was God made flesh—
God incarnate. Early Christians claim Jesus was God who "came
down" as a "servant" (Phil 2:6ff). Incarnational claims are central
to Christian theology.

It is false, however, to claim that only in and through Jesus God
became relational. God has been relating with creation, creatures, and
humans from their origins. In fact, God is not typically revealed in
Scripture with a series of claims or statements. Rather, God is revealed as
One encountered in relationships.

Let me illustrate this by telling you about someone who influenced
me: Dr. C. S. Cowles. Here are two statements that describe him:

1.   Cowles is a university professor of Bible, memorable storyteller,
     and avid hiker.
2.   Cowles wrote on my first college term paper on the Bible,
     "Outstanding Paper. It has been a privilege to have you in class—
     hope to see you again!" And he capped nearly every lecture
     by telling learners, "Close your notebook." He used the final
     moments to tell a captivating story of some hiking adventure,
     distilling important life lessons.

In the first statement, Cowles is described by professional title and
active interests. In the second, I describe Cowles in the context of his
relationship to me and to students through his storytelling.

Both statements communicate facts. But note that in the second
paragraph, I never call Cowles a professor, story-teller, or hiker. I use no

labels or titles. Rather, I narrate something about how Cowles related to students as a professor, story-teller, and hiker.

I use these statements to explore the relational theology operating within Scripture. The first portion of the Bible is profoundly relational. In this portion, we rarely read about a God with "labels" or "titles." Rather, Scripture narrates God in relationship. Perhaps the only place God receives labels and titles in any consistent way is in the Psalms. Even there, psalmists describe God with metaphors of relatedness—God is a "fortress" in relationship to the need of those who need strength.

When we think about Jewish-Christian categories for discerning God, these issues are important. In the early Scriptures, to think theologically we must think relationally. We must tell stories of God's relationship to persons or to Israel.

The New Testament also witnesses to God through stories. The Gospels use some titles for Jesus, but they do not primarily label Jesus as much as tell stories about Jesus. In these stories, we learn most about Jesus in relationship with people. In the epistles, we read less about Jesus in contextual relationship.

As the separation between Judaism and emerging Christianity grew, Christian theologians wrote fewer stories. Within Christian tradition, the focus turned to "believing" or "thinking" right things about God. Christian creeds and affirmations became central. Within Jewish tradition, however, conceptual ideas in rabbinic discourse often returned to parables and stories.

In these ways, Jewish and Christian perspectives frame unique—and connected—relational ways of thinking about God. If we were to talk to a Jew or Christian today, we might find that these historic differences between Jewish and Christian perspectives about God remain.

Ask a Christian, "Who is God?" and the Christian might answer something like this: "God is the almighty father, creator of the heavens and earth, made known in Jesus, his only Son, our Lord, conceived by the Holy Spirit ..." The emphasis falls on "titles" and creeds.

Ask a Jew, "Who is God?" and the Jew might say something like this, "Let me tell you a story ..." This Jew might begin with a genealogy to narrate a story of God's relationships with Jews from Abraham to the modern era.

Scripture has many stories. If Scripture wanted to teach us merely facts about God, the books would be much shorter, less engaging, and perhaps (I think!) more boring. But whether in story or in title, God is encountered in relationship.

I can tell you about Dr. Cowles through his titles. Or I can tell you about the relationship I have with Cowles and the relationships he has had with thousands of students. In both cases, you will learn about Cowles. But you will discern more nuance, depth, and perhaps some ambiguity if I tell you about my relationship with Cowles who remains my friend to this day. His relationship with me over time—not his titles—has shaped my entire life.

Perhaps the same is true about God as narrated in Scripture. Scripture teaches us about how God relates to persons through encounters and faithful walking with God in obedience. Early Scripture tells us about God's many relationships with many persons of faith. The New Testament is similar, but it tells us about God's unique relationship to Jesus and through Jesus to persons.

It is in the Jewish and Christian stories of God's intricate and intimate relationships—not primarily God's labels or titles—that we discern the greatest depth, wonder, and mystery about our relationship with God.

The God of Love and the Multiplicity of Religious Traditions

Mark H. Mann

If you are anything like me, you find yourself sometimes struggling to make sense of the exclusive claims of Christianity in light of the diversity of religion and life philosophies in the world. What are we to make of scriptural claims, for instance, that Jesus is the only way to God (Jn 14:6) when there are countless people who have never even heard Jesus' name? How are we to understand the fact that faithful Buddhists or Jews sometimes seem to embody the fruits of the Spirit more fully than many baptized, church-attending, Bible-believing Christians? Indeed, does not scripture state that God is more concerned about saving and reconciling lost sinners than condemning them? John 3:17 states that Christ came "not to condemn the world, but in order that the world might be saved through him." And the parable of the lost coin, the lost sheep, and the prodigal son in Luke 15 all depict God in relentless pursuit of lost sinners. How are we to make sense of all this? Speaking as a relational theologian in the Wesleyan tradition, the following are a few things that I believe *begin* to address these questions.

First, I believe that God is triune. God is three persons (Father, Son, and Holy Spirit) who share a common essence (*Nicene Creed*). This is to say that God is profoundly and fundamentally *relational* as One who possesses a complex interrelatedness.

Second, I believe that God is love (1 Jn 4:8). Since the early church, Christians have affirmed that the interrelatedness of the triune God is one of eternal, perpetual, mutual love. Father, Son, and Holy Spirit are forever held together—such that we cannot ever distinguish one from the others—in a kind of dance of love and adoration for one another. Of course, such love, as is always the case with divine love, cannot be kept to "itself." It flows outward into all of creation. Scripture suggests that such love is the very source of the universe itself!

Third, I believe that, as triune love, God lovingly creates the world in freedom. God has freely created all that is. And God has created everything to express, embody, and reflect God's own freedom. So, creation possesses a certain measure of freedom in relation to God. That is, creatures are free *because* they have been created by God to reflect and embody God's loving freedom. When we say people are "created in the image and likeness of God" (Gen 1:27), we mean in part that humans are capable of embodying and reflecting God's freedom to love.

Fourth, I believe that God is *decisively*, though not *solely*, revealed in the life, teachings, and especially the death and resurrection of Jesus Christ. Therefore, I affirm what theologians have traditionally called general revelation. That is, God, as triune, loving creator of all is continually present to and seeking to reconcile all that is fallen (Rom 8:19–21). This is, of course, the work of the Holy Spirit. We Wesleyans often speak of such revelation in terms of *prevenient grace*: the gracious work of God ever-calling all of creation to be reconciled with its creator and empowering such reconciliation (2 Cor 5:17–18; Eph 1:9–10).

This is not to say that general revelation is somehow distinct or separate from who God is revealed to be in Jesus Christ. Rather, if we take seriously the doctrine of the Trinity, as articulated above, we must affirm that the work of God in Christ and the Holy Spirit is always interrelated. God in Christ reveals to us the personality and power of the Holy Spirit, while God in the Spirit always speaks as one seeking to reconcile us and all creation to God *in Christ*. In other words, the Spirit who is present in and to all creation is constantly revealing the risen God-man (Col 1:15–20).

Another way in which we might talk about prevenient grace is in terms of God's Word being perpetually spoken to us and to all of creation. "Speaking," here, does not necessarily mean audible words communicated in a particular cross-section of physical waves we call "sound" and therefore "heard" with physical ears. Instead, God speaks in more direct and immediate ways to our hearts. How? I am not sure. But the Apostle Paul gives us a hint, I think, in Romans 8:26: "with sighs too deep for words." Consider also Genesis 1, in which God speaks numerous times and the world comes into being, or John 1, in which all creation is said to have been "spoken" into being by and through the Word of God (Christ). God has been, at all times and in all places, speaking to creation. God's Word has "gone out" into the world even where the church has not, even where Christians have yet to preach the gospel. As the psalmist declares, "Where can I go from your spirit, or where can I flee from your presence?" (Ps 139).

Fifth, even as revelation and grace are available to those who have not heard the gospel, I believe that salvation through Christ is also not limited to those who have heard the name of Jesus. Nor is it limited to those who have *explicitly* accepted Christ as Lord and Savior. Instead, I believe that many explicitly non-Christians have, by God's grace through the atoning sacrifice of Jesus Christ and the power of the Holy Spirit, come to "know" Christ in their hearts without even knowing it in their minds. Their salvation is made possible by Christ, even if they have not heard the name of Jesus. Their lives bear witness to this relationship, even if their beliefs do not. I believe that Jesus is talking about such persons in John 10:16–28. In this passage Jesus speaks of his "other sheep that do not belong to this fold" (the church) but who nevertheless "listen to his voice" and who will have "eternal life."

That there might be such "anonymous Christians" (as theologian Karl Rahner has put it) does not mean the church should stop evangelizing or sending missionaries into all the world. Quite the contrary! Just because there might be some Buddhists who are anonymously Christian does not mean that all Buddhists know Christ. Nor does it mean that even anonymously Christian Buddhists would not benefit from coming to know the One they know only in their hearts with their minds as well. Indeed, Jesus' commands us to go and make *disciples* of all nations, and Christian discipleship means coming to love and serve Christ with all of ourselves!

Initial Creation and Relational Theology

Karen Strand Winslow

The poetry and prose describing God's creation of the skies, land, seas, and all inhabitants are scattered throughout the entire Old Testament. They reveal God's continuous relationship to all that God brought into existence. Not only Genesis 1–2, but also Amos, Isaiah, Jeremiah, Psalms, and Job elaborate on God's establishment of the rain, wind, snow, mountains, seas, and land.[1] These Scriptures show that God is the loving, hopeful source and sustainer of creation.

Many of these affirmations of God's relationship with creation are consistently featured in the language of Genesis 1:1. This opening verse declares that "the maker of the sky (heavens) and land (earth)" is Israel's God, YHWH. *Because* YHWH made the heavens and earth, God's people are to believe his promises and follow his ways. *Because* God made them, they will reciprocate such love by serving their God and living at peace with one another.

From Genesis 1–2:4a and the carefully structured introduction to the story of God's intimate relationships with individuals and families, we learn that God created everything by speaking. God was pleased with the results (Gen 1:4, 12, 18, 21, and 25). A relational Subject who is present speaks other subjects into existence and names them. God calls out to light, it appears, and God names it "day." God speaks a division between the pre-light waters and names the upper set of waters "skies." God calls for the dry land to appear and names it "land." God tells the

---

1   Ps 8; 33:7; 104:5–10; 115:15; 121:2; 135:7; Job 26:7; 28:10–26; 36:27–28; 38:4–7; Am 4:13; Jer 27:5; 51:1; Is 42:5; 45:18; 37:16; Zech 12:1; see also Ex 20:11.

land to bring forth land animals. All these hear God's voice and shine, divide, order, multiply, oversee, and eat (Gen 1:29–30).

Because they hear and obey, all creation is in relationship with God. Every operation (notice the verbs!) of creation in Genesis 1 depicts the relationship between the voice of God and the responsive realities of the world. They are cooperative. The orality of God and the response of creation ground the rest of the story of God and God's people in relational terms.

God is especially pleased with how those made in God's image turn out—the male and female whom God commissioned to multiply and compassionately oversee the rest of creation (Gen 1:26–31). The creatures made most like God are told to relate to the rest of creation like the "greater light" looks after the day and the lesser light watches over the night. Male and female have a position in creation that requires their relationship with their maker and those they serve.

Genesis 1 is often said to picture God as "transcendent" or removed from creation, compared to Genesis 2 where God is pictured as more "immanent." But we should not read Genesis 1 imagining that God is distant and dispassionately commanding his creation to be good and beautiful. God's presence and voice is evidence of God's relational expectation that all aspects of creation will hear and respond.

Genesis 2 certainly pictures God relationally—even anthropomorphically. God acquired dirty hands from planting gardens and sculpting people from dirt and flesh and bone. Walking in the cool of the day, God called out to the couple who were hiding from him, because they had broken relationship by eating from the tree. Genesis 2:4b–24 (the second creation story in terms of how the Bible is ordered) is loaded with relational touches of God. God instructs the couple about how those he made should relate to Him, each other, and to the ground.

God's name here is YHWH—the personal name given to Moses to reinforce his promise to deliver Israel from Egyptian slavery—combined with "God" (Ex 3:14–15; 6:2–9). This in itself underscores God's role as hearing, aware, responding, sending, and in need of cooperative covenant partners to help bring salvation (see Ex 3:7–10).

When this story begins, we hear that there was no plant or crops, because there was no rain and no human to plow the ground. Because of this perceived need for crops, God forms a human from the mud to till the very ground from which he came. From the hands-on shaping of this human, we imagine a potter working with clay. God's breathing into this mud creature to bring him to life is among the most intimate of relational images.

God then puts away his potter's wheel and sculpting tools, pulls on gardener gloves, and picks up a spade. After planting the garden, God gives this human a job, the role of farmer.

The command to eat from all but one of the trees is another element of the relational theology that emerges from this story. The God who made him, also spoke to him (Eat this, do not eat that!) and expects obedience. But God does not force it. Obedience, which reflects love and gratitude, cannot be forced, because the nature of love requires freedom to obey.

The relational aspects of this creation story continue. When God realizes that solitude—lack of relationship—is not good for humans, He makes and personally brings all the animals to the man so he can get to know each and name it. Because no other creature made from the ground suits the man as a partner, God decides to shape a partner out of human material: bone and flesh. God pulls off his gardener gloves, puts away his shovel, and takes up instruments of an anesthesiologist and surgeon. God dons his potter's hat again to fashion and shape the woman (Gen 2:18–24).

The man recognizes her as his very bone and flesh. He names them *ish* and *ishah*—husband and wife. These terms sound alike, and this similarity depicts their inextricable relationship. Then we see where the story was going all along: marriage! God develops a relational solution for what he saw was "not good."

Later, when freedom to obey means freedom to disobey, the relational God pursues the exiles from Eden. God reminds them they could choose restoration and peace.

Creation stories and poems in the Bible illustrate God's intimate relationship to our natural environment, to our ancestors in the faith, and to us. They depict how we are interrelated—we are made of one another and for one another. We creatures are produced by the loving intentions of God who used elements that also produce the food we eat. In all this we are related to God, for we are made in his image and born by his will (Jn 1:12–13).

God's Relation to Nature

Sharon R. Harvey

Environmental action is highly politicized in this country. In fact, Christians who care about the environment are in need of theological frameworks that serve as points of navigation for environmental responsibility. Political positioning often hinders the Church from taking a stand on environmental issues. Evangelical commentators frequently disagree with global climate change, and they can give the impression that Christians prefer to support the divide between religion and science.

In the light of ecological crises, a number of questions present themselves to Christians today. For instance, is it a sin to dump toxic chemicals in the lake knowingly and willingly?

We also wonder what our responsibility might be to the animals and other creatures on our planet. Does living the holy life mean being concerned with saving furry creatures? Do these and other creatures matter to God? Is God affected by their extinction?

And what should Christians say about responsibility for the quality of soil and atmosphere? Does God care about deforestation and increased CO_2 emissions? Will we need to give an account for our lack of environmental responsibility, or are these issues just optional?

Answering these questions in light of Christian doctrine and traditional theology is not easy. Christians have not often focused on issues regarding waste management, recycling, CO_2 emissions, and other environmental concerns. Christians need resources to guide them in understanding what environmental responsibility requires today. I believe relational theology provides insights for understanding better the God/human/nature relationship.

Relational theology affirms the idea that creatures have freedom and must play a role in the work to make the world better. Some other theologies claim God is all-controlling, and they allow no place for creaturely contribution.

Many relational theologians talk about God's gracious gift of freedom to creation as an act of self-limitation. We see this self-limitation most profoundly in the incarnation, as God was in Christ related to the world and not separate from it. In Christ we find that God chooses not to control others entirely. Instead Christ acts in *kenosis*—self-emptying—and thereby is self-limited so that creatures can exercise God-given agency.

This understanding of God's power provides an important resource for thinking about the environment and ecological concerns. In fact, it can give clues about how humans ought to refrain from destroying nature and, instead, care for it.

Here are some themes in relational theology that provide resources for constructive Christian engagement with environmental issues:

1. Nature affects God. Relational theology says God relates to the world as one intimately connected with all creation. God is involved with the world, experiencing the world in ways like we experience it. Because nature affects God, it really matters to God's experience. The world matters to God.

2. All creation is interrelated and creation is ongoing. God is both Creator at the beginning and continues to create today. The creation God has made is interconnected. Creatures are not isolated from God any more than they are from other creatures and the broader environment.

3. Both the Creator and creatures are together responsible for stewarding the planet. God is active in this stewarding. But God has become self-limited, and this means God has taken a risk by giving genuine freedom to creatures. We must use this freedom wisely as covenant partners with creation.

4. We humans are called to imitate God by both stewarding and exercising self-limitation. We can voluntarily limit ourselves by refraining from excessive consumption. Humans must ponder how best to cooperate with nature and work to preserve it. We serve as partners with God in caring for the world. We can follow

the example of Jesus, who "emptied himself" and chose self-limitation for the well-being of others.

Christians must move beyond the political polarization that tempts them to ignore the charge God gives to care for creation. Relational theology can help them in this. Its emphasis upon God and humans related to nature and not entirely separate from it provides a key component in the theological work necessary for environmental responsibility. Self-limitation as a theological notion can be our humble response to the natural world, a response that can help us to sustain instead of destroy it.

Made in the USA
Middletown, DE
13 August 2020